T0323628

Cambridge Elements ≡

Elements in Public Economics
edited by
Robin Boadway
Queen's University
Frank A. Cowell
London School of Economics and Political Science
Massimo Florio
University of Milan

BENEFIT-COST ANALYSIS OF AIR POLLUTION, ENERGY, AND CLIMATE REGULATIONS

Kerry Krutilla
Indiana University, Bloomington

John D. Graham
Indiana University, Bloomington

CAMBRIDGE
UNIVERSITY PRESS

Shaftesbury Road, Cambridge CB2 8EA, United Kingdom

One Liberty Plaza, 20th Floor, New York, NY 10006, USA

477 Williamstown Road, Port Melbourne, VIC 3207, Australia

314–321, 3rd Floor, Plot 3, Splendor Forum, Jasola District Centre, New Delhi – 110025, India

103 Penang Road, #05–06/07, Visioncrest Commercial, Singapore 238467

Cambridge University Press is part of Cambridge University Press & Assessment, a department of the University of Cambridge.

We share the University's mission to contribute to society through the pursuit of education, learning and research at the highest international levels of excellence.

www.cambridge.org
Information on this title: www.cambridge.org/9781009189453

DOI: 10.1017/9781009189460

When citing this work, please include a reference to the DOI 10.1017/9781009189460

First published 2023

A catalogue record for this publication is available from the British Library.

ISBN 978-1-009-18945-3 Paperback
ISSN 2516-2276 (online)
ISSN 2516-2268 (print)

Benefit-Cost Analysis of Air Pollution, Energy, and Climate Regulations

Elements in Public Economics

DOI: 10.1017/9781009189460
First published online: May 2023

Kerry Krutilla
Indiana University, Bloomington

John D. Graham
Indiana University, Bloomington

Author for correspondence: Kerry Krutilla, krutilla@indiana.edu

Abstract: This Element offers a review and synthesis of the research on economic methods for evaluating regulations that improve air quality, save energy, and reduce climate risks. The intended audience is regulators and other constituencies interested in the nexus between scholarship and practice, analysts in government agencies and research organizations, and academic scholars and their graduate students. Topics include the evolution of regulatory impact assessment (RIA) in the OECD; cost estimation, including engineering, partial equilibrium, and general equilibrium approaches; benefit valuation, with an emphasis on the value of reducing risk of illness and premature mortality, and methods for pricing carbon emissions; discounting methods, and their relationship to carbon pricing; the distribution of regulatory costs and benefits; and uncertainty evaluation methods for addressing less and more fundamental uncertainty. A perspective on the relevance and limitations of current research is offered. This title is also available as Open Access on Cambridge Core.

Keywords: air pollution, general equilibrium, carbon pricing, social discount rate, RIA

JEL classifications: D58, D61, H23, H43, Q51, Q52, Q53, Q54, Q58.

ISBNs: 9781009189453 (PB), 9781009189460 (OC)
ISSNs: 2516-2276 (online), 2516-2268 (print)

Contents

1 Introduction

This Element focuses on benefit-cost analysis (BCA) of regulations that improve air quality, save energy, and reduce climate risks. Regulations are the dominant approach for managing environmental risks, rather than price-based instruments like carbon taxes. The distinction between quantity and price-based approaches is not always sharp, however. For example, grandfathered tradable permits can be viewed as a way to implement performance standards. The comparative properties of regulatory standards and price-based instruments are also widely studied. The Element emphasizes regulatory evaluation, but price-based policies are also considered when comparative assessment is informative for the topic at hand.

There is a well-institutionalized process for regulatory evaluation in which BCA is conducted. This process is known as "Regulatory Impact Analysis" in the United States or "Regulatory Impact Assessment" in other OECD countries (hereafter RIA). In the United States, the use of BCA for the evaluation of environmental regulations is associated with the implementation of nine major environmental statutes passed between 1969 and 1980 (Ferrey, 2013). In Europe, RIA has historically addressed the administrative burdens that regulations place on business, with environmental BCA more commonly applied to public infrastructure investments, for example, in transportation and energy. However, the use of BCA for the assessment of environmental policies and regulations is increasing throughout the OECD (Atkinson et al., 2018).

Benefit-cost analysis is inherently a tool for applied policy assessment, but it rests on a theoretical foundation in welfare economics. Conceptual approaches and trends in academic scholarship affect government guidance documents (Groom et al., 2022). Debates about methodology are common in the academic literature, and the relevance of methods and insights may not be clear to policymakers. This Element attempts to provide an integrative perspective of the academic literature, complemented with information from RIA practice. The goal is to better understand the methodology implications of the academic literature and its relationship to best practice, the gaps where more research is needed, and how RIA methodology for air, energy, and climate regulations (hereafter, AEC regulations) may evolve in the future. The intended audience is regulators and other constituencies interested in the nexus between scholarship and practice, analysts in government agencies and research organizations, and academic scholars and their graduate students.

The economic evaluation of environmental regulations is a large topic, and some limiting assumptions will guide our work. With the exception of the discussion of the Ramsey discount rate, the literature reviewed relies on the potential Pareto criterion rather than a social welfare function and distributional weighting.[1] Our review also focuses on ex ante evaluation rather than ex post appraisal. The latter has been recommended by regulatory reform proponents in recent years (e.g., Dudley and Mannix, 2018). Finally, our review focuses selectively on some key topics: specifically, regulatory cost estimation, benefit valuation, discounting, distributional assessment, and uncertainty evaluation. We hope that reviewing this swath of material within this single Element will help inform readers with a selective knowledge of some of the topics, while conveying a current view of the larger field.

Even within this demarcated scope, space constraints limit the range and depth of the coverage afforded to individual topics. Thus, our review is liberally sourced to allow readers to follow up with more detailed investigations of subjects of particular interest. Two other Elements in this series provide a general review of BCA (Johansson and Kriström, 2018) and behavioral approaches to public policy (Sunstein, 2020).

We start in Section 2 with the evolution of the RIA process. Section 3 then assesses the literature on regulatory cost estimation, considering engineering cost approaches, partial equilibrium (PE) models, and the extensive general equilibrium (GE) literature. Section 4 categorizes the benefits of AEC regulations, and then addresses two important topics in more detail: the value of reducing the risk of illness and premature death from local air pollution, and methods for pricing greenhouse gas emissions. Section 5 turns to the topic of discounting. We review the standard discounting approaches and discuss how the discounting choice is related to the method for pricing carbon emissions. Section 6 reviews the literature on the distributional effects of AEC regulations, including the distribution of regulatory costs on the supply side; the incidence of regulatory costs on consumers; the implications of the distribution of pollution rents, and the distribution of the benefits. Section 7 reviews uncertainty analysis methods relevant for AEC regulations. These include methods for valuing "less fundamental" uncertainty, as well as decision-science methods such as robust decision-making (RDM) relevant for "more fundamental" uncertainty. Section 8 summarizes and offers recommendations for future research.

2 The Evolution of Regulatory Impact Analysis

2.1 Introduction

A regulation places legal obligations or constraints on those covered, usually individuals, businesses, or other organizations in society. Regulation is different from a public investment program, where the government raises funds and uses

---

[1] See Adler (2016), Kaplow (2020), and Weisbach (2015) for insightful but contrasting views on conceptual frameworks for benefit-cost analysis.

those funds to pay the costs of the program. For a regulation, the costs of compliance are typically incurred – at least initially – by the individuals and/ or organizations subject to the regulation. Over time, regulatory costs to businesses may be passed on to consumers in the form of higher prices for products and services, or they may be paid for by diminished compensation to employees or owners of businesses.

Some regulations have strong policy rationales (e.g., civil rights protection), but the rapid proliferation of regulations in the twentieth century led to increasing concerns among businesses and the public. Critics argued that regulation was hurting the performance of the economy by contributing to inflation, reducing productivity, and curbing market innovation. Advocates of "regulatory reform" sought to eliminate unnecessary or overly burdensome regulations. When a regulation is justified, reformers promoted "smart regulation" that accomplished societal goals in ways that minimize cost and preserve as much flexibility as possible for personal and business choice.

One outgrowth of the reform movement is the requirement that regulators commission RIAs, a key element of evidence-based approaches to policymaking (Radaelli, 2020). An RIA may be undertaken before a new regulation is imposed and/or after a regulation takes effect, to ensure that the intended outcomes are achieved at reasonable cost.

The OECD defines RIA as a critical assessment of the positive and negative effects of proposed and existing regulations and nonregulatory alternatives (OECD, 2021). This definition is broader than BCA, even though BCA is a commonly used tool in RIA. Other methods include cost-effectiveness analysis, formal uncertainty analysis, scenario analysis, multiobjective decision analysis, risk assessment, and distributional analysis.

Some form of RIA is now commonplace in all OECD countries, but the practice of RIA is relatively recent in many developing countries (OECD, 2021).

2.2 Evolution of Regulatory Impact Assessment in the United States

President Ronald Reagan's 1981 Executive Order 12,291 is often cited as the origins of RIA in the United States even though presidents Gerald Ford and Jimmy Carter were both strong proponents of rigorous regulatory analysis. Executive Order 12,291 required federal agencies to prepare RIAs in support of proposed and final regulations. It also prohibited agencies from publishing proposed and final rules in the Federal Register without clearance from the Office of Management and Budget (OMB), which enabled OMB analysts to negotiate changes to rulemaking packages, including RIAs (Gray, 1998; Miller, 2011).

The Reagan administration's implementation of Executive Order 12,291 triggered substantial controversy and negative press for the Reagan White House. Critics charged that Reagan was more interested in a "relief" program for business than a constructive reform of regulatory process and policy (Eads and Fix, 1984; Olson, 1984). Some Reagan appointees at the agencies were slow to respond to legislative deadlines for new regulations.

The Reagan administration, facing a possible cutoff of funding for the Office of Information and Regulatory Affairs (OIRA), compromised by making the OIRA review process more open to public scrutiny and by agreeing to subject future OIRA administrators to a formal Senate confirmation process. Under president George H. W. Bush, the Senate did not confirm Bush's OIRA nominee, so OIRA staff worked informally with a special White House office, the Council on Competitiveness, overseen by vice president Dan Quayle. Agencies such as the Occupational Safety and Health Administration and Environmental Protection Agency (EPA) persistently resisted the efforts of OIRA staff to make changes to their RIAs and rulemaking documents. Gradually, as the unitary theory of executive power became better developed, White House regulatory review through OIRA became better accepted (Sunstein, 2012).

Under presidents Bill Clinton, George W. Bush, Donald Trump, and Joe Biden, implementation of the RIA aspects of the federal rulemaking process stabilized with some important exceptions. A Clinton executive order narrowed the OIRA review scope to "significant" regulations but granted OMB broad authority to decide which rules are significant. Clinton called for more consideration of distributional equity issues in RIA and replaced Reagan's numerical benefit-cost test with a more nuanced "benefits justify costs" test. The word "justify" is seen as allowing agencies to consider qualitative benefits and costs as well as equity issues (Katzen, 2018). Under George W. Bush, OIRA largely retained the Clinton approach but issued a technical guidance document on how to perform RIA, guidance that remains in effect today (OMB, 2003). The Obama administration emphasized the review of existing regulations and incorporated more behavioral economics into RIAs (Sunstein, 2014). The Trump administration launched an ambitious deregulatory agenda but much of this agenda was lost in court, in part due to poor-quality RIAs that did not adequately consider the foregone benefits of regulation (Belton and Graham, 2019). The Biden administration repealed the Trump administration's "regulatory budget" (aimed at spurring deregulation) but also announced it will retain the RIA process overseen by OMB. It pledged to modernize OMB Circular A-4, in part to give more emphasis to justice/equity concerns.

2.3 Evolution of Regulatory Impact Assessment in Europe

The United Kingdom and the Netherlands pioneered the "Better Regulation" agenda in Europe, leading to the European Union's eventual embrace of the agenda. The term "Better Regulation" has no universal definition but typically encompasses ex ante RIA, transparency in regulatory development, reduction of the administrative costs of regulation, consultation with stakeholders, and proportionality in the regulatory response to a problem (OECD, 2019; Wiener, 2006).

In 1985, the UK Government initiated a requirement that regulators prepare compliance cost assessments, emphasizing impacts on businesses and the economy. A broader RIA requirement, including benefits and costs, was adopted in 1998 and remains in effect today. A full RIA must accompany any proposals for primary or secondary legislation when they are proposed to the Parliament.

The Netherlands initiated business-impact studies in the 1980s. In 1994, the Dutch government called on regulators to streamline regulation "to what is strictly necessary." In the late 1990s, analysts in the Dutch government developed a new "Standard Cost Methodology" for "administrative costs" – what in the United States politicians call "red tape" or "paperwork burden." Using this metric, the Dutch government has accomplished one round of 25 percent reduction in administrative costs. However, administrative costs typically account for a small share of the overall business or societal costs of regulation, and the Dutch government is moving toward more comprehensive ex ante RIAs that quantify benefits and costs of regulatory proposals.

The European Union was slow to embrace Better Regulation until the Lisbon Agenda's emphasis on a competitive European economy in March 2000. Several years later, under the leadership of the Italian politician and economist Romano Prodi, the European Commission issued preliminary guidance on how to conduct RIAs. In 2005, under the leadership of Portugal's former prime minister, Jose Manual Barasso, the Commission instituted a mandatory RIA requirement and empowered a new Impact Assessment Board to review the quality of Commission RIAs, before they were released to the Parliament and the Council. With minor modifications, the EU process established by Barasso remains in effect today. In general, the EU embrace of RIA entailed less controversy than occurred in the United States, in part because the EU was able to learn from and respond to the US experiences (Golberg, 2018)

2.4 Comparing Regulatory Impact Assessment Requirements in Europe and the United States

The scope of the EU's RIA requirement is much broader than the scope in the United States (Wiener and Alemanno, 2010). The US RIA requirement does not apply to primary legislation considered by Congress; it applies only to the implementing regulations developed by the executive branch. In Europe, RIAs are required for all proposals of primary legislation as well as secondary legislation, regulations, directives, communications and White Papers.

On the other hand, the results of RIAs have more potential impact on decision-making in the United States than they do in the EU. The United States uses OMB as a centralized authority to ensure that regulators perform RIAs and use the results of RIAs in rulemaking. The OMB is involved in regulatory policymaking as well as analysis quality. The EU's centralized process focuses primarily on analysis quality, delving less frequently into the substance of policy making choices. As an agent of the president of the United States, OMB has more authority than the EU's centralized review body – now called the Regulatory Scrutiny Board (formerly the Impact Assessment Board). As a nationally elected politician, the president of the United States has more power than the president of the Commission, who is selected by the heads of state in Europe, and this difference reveals itself in the usually strong powers of OMB relative to US regulatory agencies (Kagan, 2001).

Judicial review of RIAs, and their use in regulatory decisions, is also a bigger factor in the United States than in Europe (Bull and Ellig, 2017). Regulatory Impact Assessments in the EU rarely play a role in litigation after a regulation is adopted but in the US RIAs are often considered in judicial review of a final regulation (Cecot and Viscusi, 2014). Through the Administrative Procedure Act, the US Congress has empowered any individual or organizations harmed by a new regulation to challenge its legitimacy in federal court, and US courts tend to encourage benefit-cost reasoning (Noe and Graham, 2019). In Europe, absent compelling circumstances, judicial review of a new regulation is available only to one or more of the twenty-eight member states of the EU (Sweet, 2003).

The technical quality of RIA is highly uneven in both the United States and Europe (Dudley and Mannix, 2018; Fraas and Lutter, 2011; Radaelli and De Francesco, 2013). The quality challenge has magnified as many of the twenty-eight member states in the EU and the fifty states of the United States have initiated RIA programs of various degrees of comprehensiveness and technical sophistication.

In the following sections, we shift from the institutional setting of RIA to the methodology issues associated with formulating regulatory BCA, particularly, BCA applied to air pollution, energy, and climate change regulations. In the United States, the benefits of AEC regulations have dominated the total benefits of the US federal regulatory program, and BCA of these regulations has generated significant political controversy and associated legal actions from environmental and industry groups. The role of BCA in the evaluation of AEC policies and regulations in Europe have been less significant than in the United States, but the use of BCA continues to advance with EU initiatives like the EU's Clean Air Policy Package and country initiatives to reduce air pollution and implement commitments under the Paris Accord.

3 Regulatory Cost Estimation

3.1 Introduction

Regulatory compliance diverts resources from other activities in the economy, imposing opportunity costs. Costs occur in the present, and also in the future when a regulation affects savings, investment, and capital accumulation. Forecasts of future regulatory impacts can also affect current-period economic adjustments.

The distributional pattern of regulatory costs affects their estimation. As noted in Section 2, regulatory costs are "off budget," falling on multiple actors in the economy. The incidence of compliance costs can be shifted, as when a polluter passes on some costs to consumers; regardless, costs are ultimately borne by the private sector without compensation.

Different kinds of regulatory costs can be identified. Direct "abatement costs" are the amount by which the costs of output increase over a given range. Partial equilibrium (PE) costs add the opportunity costs associated with output and price adjustments in the regulated market. General equilibrium (GE) costs incorporate the adjustments and feedbacks among all markets in the economy impacted by regulatory compliance.

For both practical and conceptual reasons, the scope and specificity of regulations influences the costing method. Some regulations target specific products or processes, such as appliance efficiency standards, rules governing the accidental releases of methane from natural gas pipelines, or pollution control requirements for refinery emissions. At the other end of the spectrum, regulations can apply economy-wide, such as a permit trading system used to implement a country's carbon emissions target.

For differentiated regulations of limited scope, engineering cost assessments of abatement costs is the feasible method, given data availability and limited budgets for conducting economic analyses. The proportionality requirement for RIA in the EU is less stringent than in the United States, and engineering cost estimates are likely to be used for many regulatory analyses in the EU.

Partial equilibrium models are useful when a fine-grained resolution of the regulated market is necessary for assessing the structure of regulatory alternatives and their market impacts (e.g., see Abito, 2020). Partial equilibrium modeling can also assess the dynamics of market behavior, such as regulatory effects on savings and investment, firm exit and entry, and industry concentration (e.g., Fowlie et al., 2016).

General equilibrium modeling is conceptually justified when the regulated market is linked to other markets, and these markets are distorted (SAB, 2017). Linkages result when the good produced in the regulated market is a substitute or complement to goods produced in other markets, and/or the regulation affects equilibrium conditions in input or output markets upstream or downstream in the supply chain. The welfare cost of distortions in these markets will increase or decrease as their equilibria changes, depending on the nature of the distortion and the direction of the market adjustment (Harberger, 1964).

From a conceptual point of view, linkages to distorted markets, rather than the size of the regulation, determine the relevance of GE approaches (SAB, 2017).[2] From a practical point of view, data constraints limit the specificity with which policy options and the structure of regulated markets are represented in current-generation computational general equilibrium (CGE) models, making them difficult to apply in the RIA of many kinds of regulations. The continual evolution of methods is likely to make CGE modeling more routine in RIA, building from the large academic literature that shows the significance of "second-best" welfare costs for regulatory evaluation.

We review each of these costing approaches in the subsections that follow. Costs are taken as the measurement of changes between static equilibria in the presence and absence of the regulation, or in dynamic models, between steady states or balanced growth paths. Factors are assumed to be fully employed before and after the regulation (this assumption is reconsidered in Section 6 on distributional effects). Structural rigidities in the economy that reduce the mobility of inputs, such as sector-specific capital or labor, can be reflected in this assessment, but transactions costs arising from property rights exchanges are excluded (these costs are also addressed in Section 6). The economic implications of transition paths between steady states or balanced growth paths in dynamic models are not assessed in the literature reviewed in this section.[3]

3.2 Estimating Abatement Costs

Abatement costs are derived from "engineering cost" estimates that compile the cost of each of the resources that are estimated to be used in compliance, both one time and recurring. Market prices, which are often available from surveys of

---

[2] As an illustration, comparative static analyses around the equilibrium neighborhood of the solutions to analytically solved GE models manifest general equilibrium effects for the very small changes involved.

[3] See Rogerson (2015) for the economic implications of transition paths in dynamic models.

polluters and/or vendors of pollution control equipment, are used to represent unit values.[4] Vendor prices sometimes differ from those stated by polluters, but a range of estimates can be used. In complex cases, a regulatory agency can contract with a consulting firm to provide engineering cost estimates of pollution control technologies.

Direct abatement costs are affected by the type of regulation. Technology-based standards or stringent performance standards compel particular "end of pipe" control methods such as catalytic converters or particle traps to reduce vehicular emissions, or wet and dry scrubber technologies to reduce point-source emissions. Even with the specification of technologies, however, there may be more than one compliance option. The engineering cost algorithms used in EPA's greenhouse-control RIAs for vehicular emissions contain literally hundreds of control technologies that can be combined in various ways depending on the market segment. Forecasting the cost-effective technology choices for heterogenous polluters facing a variety of technological compliance options can be difficult.

When regulations cause a technology to be used on a larger scale than the historical pattern, the supply chain of the technology may experience cost savings due to learning by doing and economies of scale. When forecasting the unit costs of mass-produced technology, the US EPA often incorporates gradual rates of savings to account for these processes.

It is not uncommon for emissions regulations to stimulate technological innovation in pollution control and / or monitoring technologies, lowering the cost of regulation. The EPA's original tailpipe standards in the 1970s induced costs due to new designs of motor vehicle engines but the performance advantages of the new engines produced nonpriced advantages that, when valued using hedonic methods, were larger than the market costs of the engines.

Experience with new technologies is not always better than anticipated. A new technology may not perform as well as vendors projected or may produce side effects that were not anticipated (e.g., sulfuric acid emissions from the early catalytic converters). Some fuel-efficiency technologies alter the way a vehicle feels when driven, and consumers have rejected some of these technologies.

Performance standards are another approach to controlling pollution. These standards impose emissions limitations without specifying the method to achieve them, offering more compliance flexibility than technology-based standards. A performance standard can limit total emissions, or the level of

---

[4] In theory, these prices should be shadow priced for economic distortions. In practice, such adjustments are often omitted.

pollution produced per unit of output or input. For example, standards can limit
the usage of energy per megawatt hour of electricity or limit the mass of
pollutants emitted per unit of energy input. These differences lead to different
economic adjustments, giving different abatement costs (Helfand, 1991).

An important justification for performance standards is asymmetric information. Polluters know more about their abatement options than regulators, giving
polluters the flexibility to exploit their private information to choose the combination of pollution control methods that minimize their costs. To comply with
an emissions standard, for example, a stationary-source polluter might increase
boiler maintenance, change boiler running times or operational conditions (e.g.,
for NO_x emissions control), or fuel switch, altering the mix of operational inputs
per unit of output. Pollution controls are another option. These cost-minimizing
choices can be difficult to forecast.[5] As with more prescriptive approaches, it is
not uncommon for analysts to make educated guesses about polluters' compliance strategies.

Incentive-based instruments like emissions taxes or tradable permits allow
the additional flexibility for cost-minimization across a population of polluters,
broadening compliance options to include differential emissions control among
them. Regulations that specify allowable air pollution concentrations over
a geographic area, usually averaged over a period of time (e.g., twenty-
four hours to one year) give the most compliance flexibility. National
Ambient Air Quality Standards in the United States offer an example of this
type of regulation. To comply with ambient standards, abatement tradeoffs can
be made among different sectors and end uses.

If priced-based policy instruments like emissions taxes or tradable permits
are implemented, the marginal costs of pollution control are revealed in the
market price of pollution. This property avoids the need to estimate abatement
costs, an important advantage in addition to the cost-efficiency of these
approaches. On the other hand, forecasting compliance modalities for ambient
air quality standards is a significant challenge. As a result, abatement cost
estimates for ambient standards come with a large uncertainty bound.

3.3 Behavioral Effects and Partial Equilibrium Costs

Direct abatement cost estimates do not reflect market responses to regulation. In
the general case, the equilibrium output level in regulated markets will decline
in response to regulatory actions. This "output substitution effect" provides an

---

[5] As an example, in the United States between 2005 and 2015, unanticipated declines in natural gas
prices (owing to the development of fracking) and growth in renewables technology displaced
coal in the fuel mix for electricity generation, reducing the anticipated cost of pollution control
(Fell and Kaffine, 2018).

additional margin for cost-minimization, lowing the social cost of the regulation (Marten et al., 2019; Pizer and Kopp, 2005). Total costs now include abatement costs on inframarginal output produced after the regulatory adjustment, and the net of producer cost savings and consumer losses over the range that output declines.

The output substitution effect depends on the degree to which the regulation increases direct abatement costs and on how the market responds. GE feedbacks affect both. In general, cost increases reflect the type of regulation and abatement options, as previously discussed, and characteristics of production processes, such as the structure of the production function, the type of inputs and their share in production, and input substitution possibilities.[6] The effect of higher costs on the output level is determined by GE supply and demand relationships when the regulated market is competitive. If the market is not competitive, the strategic behavior of polluters also becomes a variable affecting the output response. When the regulated product is traded, the world excess demand for output (which can be positive or negative) also influences market behavior (Krutilla, 1991).

The impact of regulations on market prices – regulatory cost "pass through" – under competitive and noncompetitive market structures is the subject of a large literature that studies energy price signals in response to carbon emissions restrictions; the fraction of carbon rents required to compensate the regulatory costs borne by polluters; and the effects of pricing and rent-sharing strategies on the competitiveness of regulated sectors in the international market (Fabra and Reguant, 2014; Neuhoff and Ritz, 2019; Sijm et al., 2012). Whether the market predictions in regulatory cost models – either PE or GE – are consistent with the findings of this literature could provide a useful check on modeling assumptions.

In OECD countries, concentrated industries or regulated public utilities account for a significant share of energy use, local air pollutants, and CO_2 emissions. PE models can model the structure of such markets to capture the impact of strategic producer behavior. An example is a study of policies to reduce CO_2 emissions from the cement industry in the United States (Fowlie et al., 2016). This industry is an oligopoly that faces a competitive fringe of foreign suppliers.

The study uses a dynamic infinite horizon model in which market participants compete over quantities in the present period and invest (or disinvest) in future capacity. In the present period, emissions restrictions reduce domestic output, worsening the terms of trade and the oligopolistic market distortion. In the

---

[6] In terms of regulatory design, for example, emissions standards that specify emissions per unit of input or output ("rate-based" standards) provide an implicit subsidy to output, reducing the output substitution effect (Fullerton and Heutel, 2010).

longer term, reduced profits induce firm exit from the industry, increasing market concentration. In this setting, auctioned permits are shown to impose relatively high welfare costs. Grandfathered permits impose the same short-run efficiency costs, but the prospective value loss of foregone free permits reduces the incentives for firms to exit. Pairing a border tax with a permit auction attenuates negative terms-of-trade effects while providing tariff revenue. This lowers welfare costs in the short and long run relative to permit auctioning alone. A dynamic updating scheme – the equivalent of granting permits in proportion to the firm's previous period's output – confers an output subsidy that reduces the oligopolistic market distortion and the terms-of-trade deterioration. As is the case with grandfathered permits, dynamic updating also reduces the incentive for firm exit. In all, market structure, trade adjustments, and intertemporal dynamics are shown to influence the relative costs of alternative policy designs.

3.4 Distorted Secondary Markets and General Equilibrium Modeling

Starting with research on environmental tax reforms in the mid-1990s (e.g., Bovenberg and de Mooij (1994), Bovenberg and Goulder (1997), Bovenberg (1999)), a large literature has documented the second-best welfare effects of emissions restrictions (e.g., Goulder et al. (1999), Parry and Williams (1999), Parry et al. (1999)). This research suggests that CGE modeling is necessary to trace through the linkages in the economy that affect costs when regulations impact distorted markets. The GE framework also produces conceptually correct welfare estimates, and provides an internally consistent representation of the economy, in the sense that all markets clear at all times, and all agents meet their budget constraints (SAB, 2017).

Constructing CGE models involves time and technical expertise, however, and data constraints often limit the granularity of the economic representation. To make the modeling tractable, CGE models typically aggregate consumers, production sectors, and geographic regions to a manageable number (Carbone et al., 2022). Aggregation as such does not significantly affect welfare cost estimates averaged over the entire economy (Fullerton and Ta, 2019). However, to be useful for regulatory cost estimation, models must be finely enough revolved to represent the processes or products that regulations target, and to describe the regions in which regulations are implemented if regulations differentially target specific areas, for example, those with the highest local ambient air pollution concentrations. Models should also be able to capture abatement cost heterogeneities that affect regulatory costs.

An option to address these issues is to selectively aggregate portions of the CGE model that do not need to be represented in detail, while highly disaggregating the sectors of relevance (Carbone et al., 2022). Another strategy is to incorporate highly disaggregated bottom-up or PE models within a CGE model. Methodology research on model linking is rapidly growing in the energy and climate area. So-called "soft-linking" combines models by running each of them separately, with outputs of one model serving as inputs into another. The models are run iteratively until a solution is reached. Soft-linking is a tractable way to integrate two models that are computationally burdensome even when solved alone (Krook-Riekkola et al., 2017). However, the compatibility of modeling structure is an issue when soft-linking off-the-shelf models. An alternative is to construct the bottom-up and CGE models from scratch (Andersen et al., 2019), or to "hard-link" models by integrating them completely (e.g., Helgesen et al., 2018). Hard-linking imposes computational burdens that may be insuperable. With continuing research, however, methodology advances are likely.[7]

A regulatory agency could develop a suite of models that include PE and GE models that aggregate sectors in different ways for different categories of regulatory analyses (SAB, 2017). Using different models to provide cost estimates for the same regulation would also increase information for RIA.[8]

We now turn to academic research that illustrates the insights from the GE literature on regulatory cost estimation in distorted economic settings. The first topic is second-best effect of existing taxes in capital and labor markets (the so-called tax interaction effect). This subject has received the greatest share of research. The second topic is the second-best effects associated with noncompetitive markets.

3.4.1 Effects of Tax Interactions

The impact of regulatory interventions on product prices has GE effects. These were first studied in stylized analytical and numerical GE models representing a perfectly competitive economy in which a labor tax is the only distortion in the economy (other than the regulated externality itself), for example, Goulder et al. (1999), Parry and Williams (1999), Parry et al. (1999). In this setting, if final consumption goods are substitutes for leisure, raising the relative price of consumption reduces labor supply, exacerbating

---

[7] See Bollen and Brink (2014) on modeling disaggregated abatement processes in a CGE model of air pollution policy in Europe.

[8] This idea is the spirit of using different models to provide ensemble forecasts when there are fundamental uncertainties about appropriate modeling methods (discussed in Section 7 on Uncertainty Evaluation).

the labor tax distortion. This second-best effect raises the cost of the regulation. The literature on tax interactions generally assumes that consumption
and leisure are substitutes.[9]

Using rents from emissions restrictions to finance labor tax cuts can defray
some of the extra cost from the labor market impact of the regulation, for
example, Goulder et al. (1999), Parry and Williams (1999), Parry et al.
(1999).[10] This policy approach is feasible when policy instruments capture
pollution rents, such as emissions taxes or industry-wide pollution standards
implemented via auctioned permits. Using pollution rents to finance tax cuts is
generally found to provide a smaller efficiency gain than the cost imposed by
the labor market distortion, reducing, but not eliminating, the efficiency cost
of the tax interaction.[11] An implication of these findings is that policy instruments that capture pollution rents will impose lower costs than regulatory
standards that do not raise revenue, provided the revenue is used to cut
distorting taxes.

The effects of tax distortions on the welfare cost estimates for sector-specific
regulations are explored by Marten et al. (2019). The question is whether sector-
specific regulations of $100 million or more – the common threshold in the
United States for conducting RIA – have GE effects of a magnitude that matters
for regulatory cost estimation.

To answer this question, a CGE model called "SAGE" is used.[12] It is a perfect
foresight dynamic model that simulates a horizon from 2016 through 2061,
disaggregated by nine US regions. The model represents twenty-three production sector and five consumer classes differentiated by income quintile.
Constant returns to scale production is assumed except for the natural resource
sectors, where fixed factors create upward sloping supply.[13] A putty-clay
formulation is used to differentiate capital vintages. Ad valorem taxes on
labor, capital, production, and consumption are represented in the model. In
the benchmark case, the economy evolves along a balanced growth path driven

---

[9] Specific goods can be complementary with leisure, for example, gasoline used in recreational
driving. In this case, raising the price of gasoline would reduce both fuel consumption and
leisure, attenuating the labor tax distortion, and increasing the optimal level of regulation (West
and Williams, 2007).

[10] Revenue transfers are calibrated to maintain budget balance.

[11] This result is sensitive to assumptions about the substitutability of leisure for the regulated
product (see Parry, 1997; Murray et al., 2005).

[12] SAGE stands for "Sector Applied General Equilibrium." This model has been developed by
researchers at the National Center for Environmental Economics of the US EPA. Details of the
model and its technical documentation can be found at www.epa.gov/environmental-economics/
cge-modeling-regulatory-analysis.

[13] Upward sloping supply curves decrease the pass through of prices, reducing the output substitution effect and the magnitude of efficiency costs from tax interactions (Murray et al., 2005; Bento
and Jacobson, 2007).

by exogenous productivity improvements and population growth. Economic growth also drives the government budget, which is balanced with lump sum transfers.

In the first experiment, the effects of a productivity shock equal in magnitude to an ex ante engineering cost of $100 million is simulated one-at-a-time for each of twenty-one sectors.[14] Welfare costs are compared to engineering costs for each of the sectors. Welfare costs are first measured from a counterfactual initial state in which taxes do not exist in the economy. From this baseline, the simulations show that regulatory costs are less than engineering costs for all but two sectors. For about half of the sectors, regulatory cost estimates are from 5 percent to 11 percent lower than ex ante engineering costs, and less than 5 percent lower for roughly the other half of the sectors. These results demonstrate the output substitution effect. However, when the simulations are reconducted with the economy's existing tax structure in place, the GE cost estimates are generally 15–25 percent higher than the engineering cost estimates, indicating that the efficiency costs of tax interactions dominate the output substitution effect. Sectors for which a large share of production goes to capital formation tend to be above 20 percent, reflecting the distorting effect of the capital tax on savings and investment. Simulating the impact of labor or capital taxes alone shows that the second-best cost of the capital tax is higher than the labor tax.

Other experiments include an evaluation of regulatory costs for larger regulations having an economic cost up to $10 billion, varying assumptions about elasticities, changing the input shares comprising the productivity shock, targeting regulations to new sources, and evaluating the effects of a static variant of the model. These analyses produce GE cost estimates that range from 0 percent to about 35 percent higher than ex ante engineering cost estimates, with large variance among sectors. As a point of comparison, engineering cost estimates of EPA regulations generally are assumed to be accurate within a range of plus or minus 30 percent.

The cited literature is based on cost models that do not estimate environmental benefits, or if the benefit side is modeled, environmental quality is assumed to enter utility functions separably from other goods and leisure. Environmental quality also does enter production functions. These assumptions are made for convenience, for example, due to data limitations and/or to facilitate the derivation of analytical solutions. However, the separability assumption is at odds with the utility structure assumed in the revealed preference literature for estimating environmental benefits (SAB, 2017). The absence of production

---

[14] In the base case, the productivity shock is modeled as an increase in inputs consistent with past abatement actions.

impacts is also inconsistent with literature on the productivity costs of air pollution (see Sun et al., 2017) and on the global damages from climate change (see Barrage, 2020).

The theoretical consequence of relaxing these assumptions is shown by Bovenberg (1999). When environmental quality is a close substitute for leisure in utility, improving environmental quality reduces leisure and increases labor supply. This attenuates the labor tax distortion. If environmental quality is a leisure complement, improving air quality increases leisure, worsening the labor tax distortion. When environmental quality also enters production functions, improving environmental quality increases productivity, which lowers the net-welfare cost of the labor tax distortion, ceteris paribus.

Carbone and Smith (2008) explore the effect of nonseparable utility in analytical and numerical models in which environmental quality is endogenously determined with leisure and consumption goods in a GE. In this model, feedbacks among environmental quality, leisure, and other goods affect the form of the welfare measure and the quantity equilibria that enter it. A calibrated CGE model of the US economy is used to assess the empirical significance of these interactions. As an example of the results, when a tax of 2.5 percent to 10 percent is imposed on transportation services, excess burdens are from 214 percent to 186 percent higher when environmental quality is a leisure complement than under the separability assumption. For the same scenarios, welfare burdens range from 38 percent to 51 percent of those estimated under the separability assumption if environmental quality and leisure are relatively substitutable. The disparities are less when the tax is on energy services.[15] These results suggest that substitution relationships between leisure and environmental quality can be empirically significant.

Environmental impacts on the production side have also been studied (Mayeres and Van Regemorter, 2008; Williams, 2002). The efficiency gain from reducing emissions and improving labor productivity can exactly counterbalance the usual second-best efficiency cost of substituting leisure for consumption, when production processes do not have fixed factors that earn rents (Williams, 2002). With fixed factors, however, increased productivity from lower pollution will not affect labor supply directly, and an income effect will tend to decrease labor supply (Williams, 2002).

Another case is that pollution only affects medical costs or time spent in illness. Improving environmental quality will reduce medical costs, giving more leisure time through an income effect, exacerbating the labor market

---

[15] These figures reflect the values of the parameters chosen for substitution elasticities and the other parameters in the model.

distortion. Reducing sick time gives an income effect that increases leisure, but it can also increase time that is allocated to labor. The overall effect is ambiguous (Williams, 2002).

A dynamic integrated assessment model (IAM) by Barrage (2020) includes climate damage as inputs into both utility and production. Production damage, for example, reduction of agricultural productivity, can account for up to 75 percent of the environmental damage in this model. Thus, reducing emissions and enhancing productivity has a significant effect on net welfare, attenuating some of the efficiency cost in the labor market imposed by the implementation of a carbon tax.

3.4.2 Firm Heterogeneity and Differentiated Products

The policy implications of imperfectly competitive markets and declining average cost industries are studied in the literature on international trade. One such model is by Melitz (2003), and it has been adapted in the environmental literature to closed economies with externalities. In the Melitz model, firms sell differentiated products and face monopolistic competition.[16] It is assumed that marginal production costs are constant but there are fixed entry costs. Firms do not know their productivity before entering an industry; productivity is revealed ex post as a draw from a probability distribution. In response, firms that are not productive enough to pay off their fixed costs exit the industry immediately. Discounting is ignored and variables are assumed to be unchanging over time, giving a "steady state" industry equilibrium.

Li and Sun (2015) modify this model to include a competitive clean good sector and a polluting sector that is monopolistically competitive with firms of different productivities producing differentiated products. There are no barriers to entry in the clean goods sector, but a fixed cost is incurred to enter the polluting sector. An abatement technology can be used to reduce emissions. Emissions cause disutility. An analytical model describes welfare in a steady state for an optimal emission tax and an optimal rate-based (intensity) standard that restricts emissions per unit of output. As in the model by Fowlie et al. (2016), environmental policy changes resource distributions among existing plants and alters exit and entry decisions. Rate-based standards are not as binding for higher productivity plants as for lower productivity plants, causing resources to shift to the latter. This lowers the value-weighted average productivity of existing plants. Emissions taxes do not impose this short-run efficiency cost. In the longer run, environmental policies cause lower productivity firms to exit the

---

[16] Fiscal policy distortions are not represented in this model, and the economy is endowed with a fixed labor supply.

industry, and fewer lower productivity firms to enter, with factors reallocated to more profitable firms. The distorting impact of the rate-based standard magnifies this effect. Whether the long-run efficiency benefits of the intensity standards relative to taxes overrides the short-run costs is theoretically ambiguous. A calibrated numerical model for the Canadian economy shows the efficiency effect of changing the industry composition dominants, and that emissions taxes yield lower welfare on net than emissions standards (Li and Sun, 2015).

Andersen (2018) compares the magnitude of overall welfare costs of regulations to their abatement costs in an economy with multiple manufacturing industries that differ in their pollution intensities and fixed entry costs. Again, firms are assumed to produce differentiated products under monopolistic competition. Regulations are modeled as a cost per unit of pollution; the associated resource diversion increases the marginal cost per unit of output. The regulation also creates two indirect welfare effects. Marginally profitable firms exit the industry in response to the policy, as in the Li and Sun model, which raises average productivity. However, the industry contraction also reduces product diversity, imposing a welfare penalty. The analytical model shows that welfare cost associated with diminishing product variety dominates the positive effect on average productivity, raising the social cost of regulations above abatement costs. The gap between the social cost of regulations and direct abatement costs is constant per unit of pollution abated, and reflects the elasticities of substitution across varieties and the distribution of firm productivities. Calibrating the model to a US data set, the welfare costs of local air pollution regulations under the Clean Air Act amendments for different manufacturing industries ranges from 3 percent to 20 percent higher than abatement costs. For all of manufacturing, marginal welfare costs are 9 percent higher than abatement costs.

4 Benefits of Air, Energy, and Climate Regulations

4.1 Introduction

In this section, we focus on the benefit side in RIA. The standard approach is to model the link between regulatory interventions and health or environmental outcomes and then to apply unit values to the outcomes, giving total benefits. Market prices, market-derived shadow prices, or benefit transfers, such as the value of statistical life (VSL) or the social cost of carbon (SCC), are typically used to represent unit values.

This standard approach estimates the benefits outside the economic model that generates the costs. This dichotomy has conceptual limitations. Including environmental goods with other goods nonseparably in utility in a CGE model would give a theoretically correct demand system for all goods, reflecting GE feedbacks and the economy's budget constraints (SAB, 2017). Benefit valuations derived within such a model are likely to differ from those conventionally estimated. For example, the standard approach relying on constant unit values implies nondeclining marginal valuations, which is inconsistent with demand theory. Conventional approaches also pose the risk of double counting, if the scope of different benefit categories is not clearly delineated.

It may be more feasible to specify the impacts of morbidity in CGE models than preferences for mortality risk reduction, see for example, Mayeres and Van Regemorter (2008). As a longer-term goal, a scientific advisory board of the US EPA recommends representing environmental goods nonseparably in utility and calibrating preferences for mortality risk aversion in EPA's numerical GE models (SAB, 2017). To be useful for valuing the benefits of many types of regulations, CGE models would also need to be disaggregated, or linked to other models, to represent policy-relevant spatial heterogeneities, such as local exposure risks and demographic characteristics.

In the remainder of this section, we stick with the conventional practice and, given space constraints, limit the scope of this review. In the next subsection, we overview the pathways that give rise to the benefits of AEC regulations. We then turn to two benefit categories that have received significant attention from researchers and policymakers: the value of reducing risks of illness and premature death, and the value of reducing greenhouse gas emissions. Primary valuation methods are not common for regulatory evaluation and are not considered here.[17]

4.2 Benefit Valuation Pathways

Figure 1 shows the various pathways for benefits arising from AEC regulations. Energy efficiency regulations or climate policies like carbon emissions standards reduce greenhouse gases (arrow 1). Air pollution regulations that reduce local or regional exposures to black carbon also reduce the risks of climate change (arrow 2). The value of carbon emissions reductions are monetized using the SCC or target-consistent carbon prices (TCPs). Other greenhouse gases typically are monetized from their carbon equivalent (discussed in Section 4.4).[18]

Energy savings are another benefit category from energy efficiency or climate regulations (arrow 3). In most RIAs, market prices are used to value these

---

[17] For a review of primary valuation methods, see Atkinson et al. (2018). See Haab et al. (2020) on the state of the art for contingent valuation; Johnston et al. (2017) on best practices for stated preference methods; Bateman and Kling (2020), Bishop et al. (2020), and Evans and Taylor (2020) on best practices for revealed preference methods; and Knetsch (2020) for the implications of behavioral psychology for public goods valuation.

[18] Productivity impacts dominant the benefits of reducing greenhouse gas emissions. Barrage (2020) finds that productivity effects account for up to 75 percent of the damage of a 2.5°C rise in global temperature.

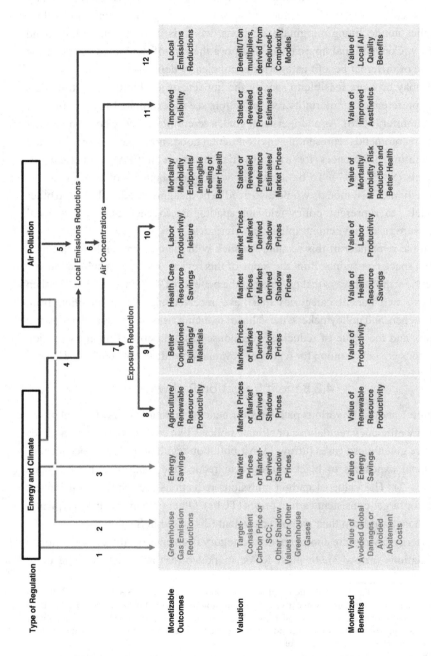

Figure 1 Benefit valuation pathways

benefits, sometimes with adjustments for "rebound effects" and/or market distortions (HM Treasury, 2021; Krutilla and Graham, 2012).[19]

Air pollution is reduced when fossil-fuel combustion declines or regulations target emissions directly. Thus, energy and climate regulations can reduce local or regional air pollution as a co-benefit (arrow 4), while reductions in local air emissions are the primary effect of air pollution regulations (arrow 5). A Chemical Transport Model (CTM) is commonly used to map air emissions reductions at local sources into pollutant concentrations at local receptors (arrow 6). Concentration- or exposure-response functions are then used to translate changes in air pollutant concentrations or exposures into health or environmental effects (arrows 6/7-8; 6/7-9; 6/7-10).

The left-most branch for "Exposure Reduction" indicates the impact of local air quality on agriculture and other renewable resources (arrow 8), for example, ground-level ozone impacts agricultural productivity (Hong et al., 2020; Sun et al., 2017). Air pollution also damages materials, buildings, and historical sites (Rabl, 1999; Spezzano, 2021) (arrow 9). Market prices or market price-derived shadow prices are usually used to monetize the benefits of reducing these impacts.

Exposure reductions also provide a variety of benefits associated with improving human health (arrow 10). Health care resource savings are generally monetized with market prices, or in some cases shadow prices that remove price markups (Drummond et al., 2015). Health improvements also increase labor productivity and affect utility directly (Mayeres and Van Regemorter, 2008). Wage rates are typically used to value productivity gains. In applied work, the value of leisure is sometimes monetized as fraction of wage rates. But because time savings are important in wide variety of economic contexts (e.g., transportation and recreation) there is large literature on estimating the value time, for example, Dalenberg et al. (2004), Jara-Diaz et al. (2008).

Reducing air pollution exposures reduces a variety of morbidity endpoints including chronic bronchitis and nonfatal heart attacks. These can be monetized using market prices, market price-derived shadow prices, or using stated preference methods, for example, Viscusi et al. (1991). The effect of a regulation on premature mortality is monetized using the VSL, as discussed in the next subsection.[20]

The direct utility effect of reducing air pollution haze and increasing visibility is another possible benefit of controlling air emissions (arrow 11). The stated

---

[19] The rebound effect is an "output substitution" effect that works in the opposite direction of the output substitution effect described in Section 3. Improving energy efficiency reduces the cost of a vehicle mile traveled (VMT). This tends to increase VMT, partially offsetting the energy efficiency gain.

[20] Reducing mortality risks is quantitatively the most important benefit associated with air pollution regulations in the OECD (Friedrich, et al., 2001). Similar figures are found for other countries (Narain and Sall, 2016). In the United States, reducing mortality risks from one pollutant, PM2.5,

preference literature describes the valuation of this difficult-to-quantify benefit, for example Boyle et al. (2016).

The right-most branch of the figure shows a way of deriving air pollution-related health benefits that avoids the regular use of CTMs (arrow 12). CTM simulations are time intensive, and technical and/or resource limits constrain the use of CTMs. An alternative is to rely on reduced complexity models that give benefits per unit of emissions reduced. These models use response surfaces, regression analysis, or other methods to link emissions reductions at sources to concentrations at receptors (Gilmore et al., 2019). The changes in concentrations are converted into benefits in the standard way, that is, using exposure-response functions, and valuing the benefits. Relating the benefit estimates to the emissions reductions gives a benefit per unit multiplier. Once these multipliers are compiled, they can be directly applied to source-specific emissions reductions to give receptor-area benefits.

Figure 1 indicates that AEC regulations generate a multiplicity of benefits. An additional channel for co-benefits is related to the technical fact that pollution control technologies can reduce more than one pollutant. For example, baghouse filters entrain pollutants based on size, regardless of type or chemical composition. Regulations targeting one kind of pollutant, for example, mercury emissions, can also reduce others, such as PM2.5. Different pollutants present different health risks, and to the extent practical, the benefits of all emissions reductions should be monetized (Driscoll et al., 2015; Markandya et al., 2018). However, itemizing co-benefits can lead to double counting if nonexclusive valuation methods independently generate the benefit estimates. Thus, care needs to be taken in the aggregation of co-benefits.

Quantifying and measuring this diverse array of benefits poses methodology and data challenges. Given space constraints, we focus on just two topics in the remainder of this section that have generated significant attention in the literature: (1) the value of reducing the risks of illness and premature death, and (2) the value of reducing greenhouse gas emissions.

4.3 Economic Value of Reducing Risk of Illness and Premature Death

We begin with the harder case of lifesaving benefit, and then consider the seemingly more tractable case where the frequency (or severity) of illness is reduced, without any impact on longevity.

---

commonly accounts for 95 percent to 99 percent of the total value of air pollution regulations (Smith and Gans, 2015).

Beginning with the insights of Schelling (1968) and Jones-Lee (1976), the approach has been to determine the willingness to pay (WTP) of the affected public for the risk reductions, and those WTP estimates become the primary economic measure of the health benefit for use in BCA. The risk evaluation does not resemble WTP for saving an identified life, such as a trapped coal miner or a patient in urgent need of kidney dialysis. Instead, analysts need estimates of the WTP to protect anonymous citizens that will experience statistical reductions in their probabilities of death and serious illness when exposures to pollution decline.

It turns out that people are willing to pay a substantial amount for such a seemingly small reduction in annual mortality risk, for example, to reduce the average risk of PM-related death from 8 chances in 100,000 to 7 chances in 100,000 per year, or an incremental reduction of 1 chance in 100,000 per year. In the United States, those values have played an important role in making an economic case for environmental regulation (Graham, 2008).

Two approaches have been used to measure the public demand for risk reduction in monetary units. First, economists measure the revealed preferences of workers and consumers when they confront mortality risks in daily decisions. This literature, which has exploded worldwide in the last forty years, finds that avoidance of a 10(−5) annual mortality risk is valued, on average, at $100 - per year in the United States and by smaller amounts in countries with lower average incomes (Hammitt and Robinson, 2011; Viscusi, 2018) Second, economists measure the stated preferences of respondents who are asked questions that entail making tradeoffs between money and mortality risks. The results of the stated preference studies also suggest significant WTP for mortality risk reductions but the magnitudes of the estimates may be significantly smaller than the revealed preference estimates (Navrud and Lindhjem, 2011).

The VSL is a summary measure used to describe estimates of the economic value of lifesaving. Suppose a population of 100,000 individuals is each exposed to a 10(−5) mortality risk. Risk analysts say that 1 "statistical life" is at stake. A VSL value of $10 million implies that the 100,000 individuals, together, are willing to pay $10 million to avert the statistical death, or an average of $100 per individual. In the United States, federal regulatory agencies are now using VSL estimates around $10 million while some European countries tend to use smaller VSL values from $1 to $5 million. The smaller VSL values outside the United States reflect at least two factors: smaller per capita incomes and greater reliance on the stated preference method of valuation.

The current estimate of VSL used in the United States is based on the mean of a fitted distribution of twenty-six estimates of VSL from studies conducted between 1974 and 1991. Five of the studies are stated preference studies and twenty-one are hedonic wage studies. The EPA is in the process of determining whether a revision of this estimate is needed. There is continuing research on the value of the VSL, updating past studies or applying new methods (see Robinson and Hammitt, 2016).

One question is whether VSL should be a constant value or vary according to the disease context and the characteristics of the population. Research suggests that the value is heterogeneous (Greenberg et al., 2021; Viscusi, 2010). The economics literature supplies evidence that VSL varies by cause of death (e.g., higher for cancer than traumatic injury), by age of the affected population (e.g., high for children, highest in the middle of the lifespan, and declining slowly after the age of sixty-five), by income and wealth, and by other factors. However, regulatory agencies tend to use uniform VSL values, perhaps fearing that valuing some subgroups less than others raises sensitive ethical and political issues. In an environmental context where pollution reduction may extend life only slightly toward the end of the lifespan, some analysts argue for a different metric: the value of statistical life year (VSLY). The VSLY may still be quite large, say $300,000 per year in the United States, since elderly citizens may value their remaining years of life highly and may have accumulated substantial assets to support their WTP for additional longevity.

One of the reasons that VSL is not a constant is that some ways of dying are associated with a longer period of morbidity, and more pain and suffering, than others. The revealed preference literature suggests that this period of suffering prior to death is not unimportant but the majority of the VSL value is attributable to the fact that life ends prematurely (Gentry and Viscusi, 2016).

Some environmental regulations reduce the risk of morbidity (e.g., bouts of bronchitis from inhalation of air pollutants) without changing mortality probabilities. Different values of statistical injury (VSI) are available for illnesses of different durations and severity (Cameron, 2014). For a nonfatal illness that is associated with an extended hospital stay and some posthospital recovery time, the average VSI may be as high as $300,000 to $500,000 per case, or about 3 percent to 5 percent of the average VSL value (Gentry and Viscusi, 2016).

Many of the benefits of reducing nonfatal illnesses are experienced by the people affected by the illness. They will presumably account for those private impacts in either their stated or revealed preference measures. There are also external costs of nonfatal illnesses that can be substantial. They include foregone production that disrupts employers and payments for health care resources that are made by the government or by private insurers with imperfect risk pools. Some of these external impacts also occur with premature death and ideally should be included in a full accounting of health benefits (UK, 2016).

4.4 Pricing Greenhouse Gas Emissions

Pricing greenhouse gas emissions is commonplace in OECD countries. There are two basic methods: the SCC and the TCP. The SCC is the discounted present value of the stream of damage resulting from this period's emission of one metric ton of carbon (or CO_2). The SCC is used for regulatory BCA in the United States, Canada, and Germany (US GAO, 2020). In contrast, the TCP is the cost of reducing the marginal ton of carbon along a trajectory to a carbon emissions target, or global temperature limitation. The TCP is used in France and, since 2009, in the United Kingdom (US GAO, 2020). The TCP approach is consistent with implementation of a least-cost strategy for achieving the targets specified in the Paris Climate Accord.

4.4.1 The Social Cost of Carbon

The SCC is estimated using an IAM that combines a model of the global economy with a biogeophysical model of the global climate system. The model is used to forecast a business-as-usual CO_2 emissions trajectory and associated climate indicators. The climate response is translated into monetized economic costs using damage functions. One metric ton of carbon is then added in the present period, and the incremental stream of environmental damage forecast. The discounted present value of the incremental damage gives the SCC. Models with stochastic components generated expected SCCs or SCC distributions.

Three IAMs are foundational in the literature: The Dynamic Integrated Climate and Economy (DICE) model; the Climate Framework for Uncertainty, Negotiation, and Distribution (FUND) model; and the Policy Analysis of the Greenhouse Gas Effect (PAGE) model. From 2010 to 2016, ensemble forecasts from these models were used to establish SCC estimates for regulatory analysis in the United States.[21] A national academy report in 2017 recommends an alternative approach based on the modularization of key IAM components (NAS, 2017).

The academic literature on IAMs is robust. Starting with Golosov et al., (2014), a series of studies have developed reduced complexity IAMs that can be analytically solved, giving "simple rules" for the SCC.[22] At the same time, complex numerical IAMs have been developed providing greater resolution of the global economy and the climate system, and their dynamical interactions (e.g., Lontzek et al., 2015). More accurate representations of the science of climate processes are being incorporated into IAMs (Dietz and Venmans, 2019).

---

[21] See Metcalf and Stock (2017).   [22] See Withagen (2022) for a review of these models.

Research on the relationship between temperature change and economic damage is also increasing, for example, Burke et al. (2015).

The impact of economic and scientific uncertainties on SCC estimates is another area of growing research (e.g., Lontzek et al., 2015; van den Bremer and van der Ploeg, 2021). Models are incorporating the effects of catastrophic damage arising from tipping points and regime shifts, for example, positive feedbacks between global warming and the carbon cycle, and effects of rapidly diminishing ice sheets (Dietz et al., 2021, Lontzek et al., 2015).

Weighting global damage by income disparities is also the subject of academic research. Distribution-weighted SCCs require projecting growth rates and making judgments about both intragenerational and intergenerational equity (Anthoff and Emmerling, 2019). A weighted-SCC approach is used by the German government for pricing CO_2 emissions (US GAO, 2020).

The effects of greenhouse gases other than CO_2 are commonly estimated using their greenhouse gas warming potentials (GWPs). Applying a GWP gives the number of tons of carbon that has the same warming effect as one ton of the source greenhouse gas.[23] This method provides a linear approximation that may understate global warming effects, given nonlinearities in the radiative forcing of different greenhouse gases, and their different atmospheric residence times (which affects discounted present values) (see Waldhoff et al., 2014.) In 2016, the United States developed estimates for the social cost of methane (SCM), and research on the SCM and nitrous oxides is ongoing.

The SCC, or the equivalent for other greenhouse gases, is derived from optimizing social welfare assuming that climate damage is the only externality, giving optimal emissions trajectories. Emissions trajectories can also be optimized in the presence of binding environmental constraints, or values of parameters can be tested to see which give optimal emissions trajectories consistent with temperature limitations or emissions constraints, for example, Dietz and Venmans (2019). Hänsel et al. (2020) update the calibration of DICE model to better represent the carbon cycle and energy balance model, and environmental damage estimates. They also include the results of an expert elicitation on discount rates (Drupp et al., 2018). This model shows that 75 percent of optimal carbon emissions trajectories fall within the 2°C target for peak warming established in the Paris Agreement.

---

[23] Carbon budgets in the UK are based on a "carbon equivalent target" where GWPs are used to convert greenhouse gases into their tons-of-carbon equivalent (HM Treasury, 2021).

4.4.2 The Target-Consistent Carbon Price

An alternative is to use carbon prices to steer an economy along the least-cost path to an emissions target, such as net zero emissions, or to keep the economy under a temperature limitation, such as those specified in the Paris Climate Accord. To implement climate policies at the country level, the target emissions over which a country has jurisdiction is the practical performance objective.

To implement the target-consistent approach, a relatively near-term emissions target is specified, for example, for the year 2050, and an emissions trajectory is characterized that is expected to attain it. The abatement schedule can be shifted earlier or later in the target time period; views differ about the recommended trajectory (see Kaufman et al., 2020; Stern et al., 2022). Economic modeling is used to estimate the carbon price evolution necessary to achieve the emissions trajectory, considering expected trends in technology, population, energy use, and other policies affecting emissions. Carbon prices and/or emissions targets can be updated with new information.

Models generally assume myopic expectations, rather than using perfect foresight (or rational expectations) as is common in the IAM literature (Kaufman et al., 2020). This implies that times paths specified are not likely to be intertemporally efficient, as measured in an infinite horizon optimization model (see, Dietz and Venmans, 2019).

If a cap-and-trade program is linked to the emissions target, the price of permits is the relevant carbon price. This situation is evolving in the EU, as the sectoral coverage of the European Emission Trading System expands.

4.4.3 Comparison of the Two Methods

The SCC and the target-consistent carbon pricing approach implicitly reflect different normative perspectives about standing to make judgments about intergenerational equity, and different views about the best way to integrate economics and science to support climate policymaking. Using the SCC approach, choices about intergenerational tradeoffs are embodied in the selection of the discount rate and, with this decision made, regulatory BCA determines the level of emissions control. The benefits of emissions control, as measured by the SCC, are summed with other benefits of a regulatory proposal, and if the total benefits exceed the total costs, emissions are reduced. The goal is to move the economy in the direction of an economic optimum. This approach reflects confidence that IAMs can predict economic behavior and climate responses accurately enough to provide informative carbon prices (see Metcalf and Stock, 2017).

In the target-consistent approach, normative judgments about intergenerational equity are made through a deliberative process that establishes the emissions targets and corresponding emissions trajectory.[24] Government officials in the United Kingdom interviewed for a report by the US GAO viewed the target-consistent approach as a precautionary stance, in the sense that the use of the TCP ties decision-making to emissions targets, which might not be attained using the SCC approach (US GAO, 2020). In this conception, the emissions target might be viewed as a "safe minimum standard" (see Toman, 2017), with the TCP the mechanism to keep a country on the right side of the "safe minimum." Regulatory benefit-cost analyses using the TCP provide an economic measure of the degree to which a regulatory proposal burdens or benefits the emissions cap. The resulting costs for additional emissions or cost savings for emissions reductions are incorporated into the overall economic evaluation of the regulatory proposal.

An issue in the comparative assessment of carbon pricing approaches is the uncertainties in the IAM forecasts that generate estimates of the SCC, and whether the growing literature that addresses uncertainties provides credible ranges for use in RIA. The SCC estimates are sensitive to discount rates, climate sensitivity (the response of surface temperatures to changes in atmospheric CO_2), and estimates of environmental damages (Pindyck, 2017). The appropriate discount rate is debated in economics, although some consensus about consumption discount rates for climate policy modeling is emerging.[25] Climate sensitivity is affected by dynamically complex feedback processes that are likely to change with rising temperatures (Roe and Baker, 2007). Some scientists believe that the mechanisms and consequences of these processes are fundamentally unknowable (Allen and Frame, 2007). Pindyck suggests that the damage functions in IAMs lack theoretical or empirical justification, and in fact, that the damage impacts from climate change, like the processes of climate change, may be fundamentally unknowable (Pindyck, 2013, 2017).[26] He suggests an alternative SCC approach based on the emissions reductions necessary to avoid catastrophic risks, defined as a reduction in GDP of 20% or more. Expert judgments are solicited for estimates of the annual growth rate of emissions under a business-as-usual scenario over a defined horizon. Respondents are also queried about the probability of various GDP reductions associated with the expected baseline carbon emissions trajectory, and to

---

[24] See Morgan et al. (2017) for an example of such a process.

[25] An expert survey by (Drupp et al., 2018) showed 90 percent of values varied between 1 percent and 3 percent, with a mean of 2.3 percent. A survey by Pindyck (2019) indicated a mean discount rate of 2.6 percent.

[26] Anticipating future adaptation is one component of this uncertainty.

provide estimates of the average emissions growth rate required to prevent a GDP reduction of 20 percent or more (Pindyck, 2019). The "average" SCC is measured as the discounted stream of expected GDP losses avoided over a time horizon, divided by the discounted stream of emissions reductions required to prevent the losses.

Stern et al. (2022) criticize the first-best optimization framework of IAMs that represents global warming as the only externality. They catalogue numerous other distortions that should influence the SCC, including imperfect or missing markets for risk; externalities in research and development, innovation, and technology; network externalities; constraints on government policy; and adjustment costs, among others. In view of these distortions, and the fundamental uncertainties associated with climate change, Stern et al., (2022) support the target-consistent method as a precautionary approach for limiting global temperature changes within reasonably safe limits.

Of course, modeling target-consistent abatement cost trajectories is not without uncertainty. And Section 3 suggests that estimating abatement costs in distorted economies is not trivial. This is not a comparative disadvantage, however, given that IAMs ignore these distortions. In an ideal world, the evolution of permit trading systems tied to emissions targets would avoid the cost estimation task altogether (assuming shadow pricing for the distortions is not considered). As noted, this type of policy is developing in the EU.

5 Discounting for Regulatory Evaluation

5.1 Introduction

The social discount rate (SDR) is the threshold rate of return required to justify public projects or policies. It is used to generate weights ("discount factors") that decline over time.[27] Applying these weights converts future benefits and cost streams into their present value equivalents. Present value equivalents are commensurable with initial period costs, enabling a temporally consistent benefit-cost comparison.

Two SDR concepts are discussed in the discounting literature, the social opportunity cost of capital (SOC) and the consumption discount rate (CDR). The SOC represents the private rate of return foregone when a policy displaces investment. The CDR is the consumer's marginal willingness to trade current for future consumption; it measures intertemporal opportunity costs when a policy displaces consumption. The CDR can be derived from market data or using the Ramsey discounting formula.

---

[27] Unless otherwise stated, it assumed that the discount factors are based on a constant per period rate of return. For insights about declining discount rates, see Laibson (1997).

As is commonly pointed out, different discounting approaches converge to the same rate in an economy with perfect capital markets. In actual markets, risk premia, taxes on capital returns, and taxes on the interest earnings of savers create wedges between pre- and after-tax returns. Credit rationing and risks also differentiate credit market segments. These market characteristics give rise to different discount rates, requiring a choice about the appropriate discount rate for public policy.

Discounting methodology must also address uncertainty of various kinds. These include nondiversifiable systematic risks affecting regulatory performance, such as positive correlations between benefits and economic growth, as well as uncertainties about economic growth processes, discount rates, and rare catastrophic events (Gollier, 2013; Groom et al., 2022). Unless otherwise noted, this section abstracts from systematic risks to consider other types of uncertainty.

Uncertainties are particularly pertinent for climate regulations. Capital markets provide diminishing information as time horizons increase,[28] long-range forecasts have limited precision, and intergenerational tradeoffs raise philosophical questions. Moreover, exponential discounting greatly reduces the present values of longer-term returns. For example, the DICE model estimates that the 2025 value for the SCC drops from \$140/ton to \$22.6/ton as the discount rate rises from 2.5 percent to 5 percent (Nordhaus, 2017). These issues make the choice of intergenerational discount rates especially challenging.

We now turn to the main topics of this section.[29] The next two subsections describe the market-based and Ramsey rule derivations of the CDR, before turning to the SOC discounting method. The next subsection addresses the discounting implications of the incidence of regulations on consumer credit markets. The final subsection describes the appropriate discount rate when intragenerational efficiency and intergenerational equity are separated as policy objectives.

5.2 The Market-Based CDR

Savers who invest in low-risk government securities receive a relatively stable after-tax rate of return. This return compensates the investor for the value of current consumption foregone and is commonly used as the CDR.[30] Capital

---

[28] The US government does not offer bonds with maturities greater than thirty years. The governments of some other countries, for example, Austria, France, Switzerland, and the United Kingdom sell bonds with maturities up to fifty years. (Christensen et al. 2021)

[29] The discounting literature is too vast to comprehensively summarize here. See Groom et al. (2022); Gollier and Hammitt (2014); Florio (2014), and Harrison (2010) for general reviews. See Cropper et al. (2014) on declining discount rates, and Gollier (2013) for Ramsey rule extensions.

[30] The "real rate of return" above the level of inflation is the appropriate discount rate for policy evaluation.

taxes and taxes on interest paid to savers vary throughout the OECD, giving different after-tax returns (hence, different CDRs) on low-risk government securities.

The size and liquidity of bond markets provide the empirical benefit of reliable data (CEA, 2017). However, a limitation of using bond markets as the basis for the CDR is that a large fraction of the public does not hold government debt.[31]

Rates of return on government securities have a term structure. Returns on a ten-year treasury bond are the basis for the 3 percent CDR recommended in OMB Circular A-4 in the United States (OMB, 2003). Real bond yields in OECD countries have declined in the last two decades. In the United States, the real yield on ten-year treasury notes is beneath 2 percent (CEA, 2017). The decline in real bond rates has led to recommendations to lower the CDR for US regulatory evaluation (Carleton and Greenstone, 2021).

The CDR is recommended in the guidance documents of the European Union and a number of European countries (see Florio, 2014; Groom et al., 2022). These CDRs are calibrated from rates earned on government securities but also using the Ramsey discounting rule. Consumption discount rates range between 1 percent (Germany) and 4 percent (Ireland). Like the United States, Denmark uses both the CDR and the SOC as the basis for regulatory evaluation.

CDRs in the United Kingdom and European countries frequently decline as step functions over time (Danish Finance Ministry, 2019; Groom et al., 2022). Circular A-4 in the United States allows for a lower, constant discount rate for regulations having intergenerational effects. Intergenerational welfare is a common motivation for low or declining discount rates. However, "certainty-equivalent" discount rates decline over time when the discount rate itself is uncertain. This occurs when discount rates are constant over time but uncertain, or when the discount rate is not fixed over time, but the stochastic process perpetuates disturbances (Newell and Pizer, 2003).

The certainty-equivalent rate can be computed as an average over a time horizon or as an instantaneous rate at a given time.[32] To illustrate, assume there is an equal probability of a 3 percent or 7 percent discount rate in all time

---

[31] The latest federal reserve data for the United States (2019) indicates that 7.5 percent of consumers held savings bonds and 1.1 percent invested in directly held bonds. Federal Reserve (The Fed - Chart: Survey of Consumer Finances, 1989 - 2019 (federalreserve.gov)).

[32] When the discount rate is a random variable, a certainty-equivalent discount rate is the rate that gives the same value for the discounting factor as the expected value of the discounting factor. Let R_t be the certainty equivalent rate, r_t be a random variable for the discount rate at moment t, and p_t be the expected discount factor. Then, $\exp(-R_t t) = E(\exp(-r_t t)) \rightarrow R_t = -\frac{1}{t}\ln(p_t)$, where R_t is an average from period t to 0. The instantaneous certainty equivalent rate is given by: $\frac{dp_t/dt}{p_t}$. These derivations are from Cropper et al. (2014).

periods. In this case, the average and instantaneous certainty-equivalent rates at fifty years are 4.13 percent and 3.48 percent, respectively. At 100 years, the corresponding rates are 3.68 percent and 3.07 percent. In the long run, the certainty-equivalent rate declines to the lower bound of the distribution. The convexity of the discounting factor, and a property described by Jensen's inequality, account for this result (Cropper et al., 2014).

5.3 The Ramsey Discounting Approach

The Ramsey discount rate is used in BCA in the United Kingdom and a number of European countries (Groom et al., 2022). It is also used for project evaluation in the EU when financing is sourced from structural adjustment funds (Florio, 2014).

The Ramsey rule is based on a utilitarian welfare function. A social planner maximizes intertemporal welfare over an infinite horizon, with utility in each moment t represented as an increasing and strictly concave function of average (per capita) consumption, $U(c_t)$. The utility function is assumed to be time invariant, and utilities across time are assumed to be additively separable. An isoelastic utility function, $U(c_t) = \frac{c_t^{1-\eta}}{1-\eta}$, is commonly used.[33] The term, $\eta = -\frac{cU_{cc}}{U_c} > 0$, denotes the absolute value of the elasticity of the marginal utility of consumption, and is constant in the isoelastic specification. The higher the value of η, the more concave the utility function. This implies more rapid decline in marginal utility $(c_t^{-\eta})$ over time, if consumption is growing, and therefore, an increasing willingness to smooth consumption. It also implies greater aversion to intra-temporal income disparities and, when project outcomes are modeled as uncertain, greater risk aversion.[34]

Given a utility discount rate, ρ, and growth rate of consumption, g, maximizing intertemporal welfare yields the optimality condition: $r = \rho + \eta g$. At the margin, this rule equates the rate of return on savings, r, with the rate of return on consumption $(\rho + \eta g)$. The expression $\rho + \eta g$ is the standard Ramsey discount rate, providing the basis for calibrating the CDR from the ρ and ηg components. The term, ηg, shows the marginal value of consuming now rather than later, given $\eta > 0$ and the (default) assumption that $g > 0$.

In the context of intergenerational discounting, the term $\rho + \eta g$ can be interpreted as a normative rule for trading societal welfare over long horizons. In this case, the value for ρ is based on an ethical view about the degree to which future utilities should be discounted – it is commonly set to zero – while the

---

[33] When $\eta = 1$, $U(c_t) = \ln(c_t)$

[34] Preference can be specified that separate out the risk aversion and other components of η. See Lontzek et al. (2015) and van den Bremmer and van der Ploeg (2021) for examples.

η term becomes a distributional weight indicating intertemporal inequality aversion. The ηg term shows the rate of return required to compensate current consumption sacrifices when future generations are consuming more (assuming $g > 0$), and the marginal utility of future consumption is declining.

Given its welfare theoretic origins, the Ramsey discount rate is commonly described as "prescriptive" or "normative." However, the Ramsey rule is interpreted in different ways in the literature. Some scholars suggest that the Ramsey discount rate should be consistent with a riskless, real market rate of interest, for example, Weyant (2008).[35] Others argue that the ρ and η parameters should be regarded as purely normative and, therefore, that the Ramsey discount rates cannot be expected to correspond to market rates (Sterner and Persson, 2008). Still others argue that the parameters of the Ramsey discount rate should be consistent with the public's preferences. This is the approach taken by the British Government (Groom and Maddison, 2019). Newell et al. (2022) use a hybrid approach recommended in NAS (2017) in which the forecasted values of the CDR are based on Ramsey components that are calibrated to give CDRs consistent with short-term market rates.[36]

The Ramsey rule can be extended in a variety of ways (see Gollier, 2013). One is to incorporate uncertainties about expected growth. If the utility function is isoelastic, and logarithmic growth is independent and identically normally distributed, $\ln(\frac{c_t}{c_o}) \sim N(\mu, \sigma^2)$, an extended Ramsey rule can be written as $r = \rho + \eta g' - \eta(1 + \eta)\sigma^2$, with g' the expected consumption growth rate. The third term introduces "prudence" (denoted by $(1 + \eta)$) and the volatility of future income, σ^2, which in combination, lead to precautionary behavior that lowers the discount rate by a constant amount (Gollier and Hammitt, 2014).

Shocks to economic growth are likely to be positively correlated and, in this case, the persistence of the shocks magnifies future uncertainty, increasing the precautionary saving motive. Using an isoelastic utility function, this causes the discount rate to decline over time. Discount rates will also decline when the growth process is independent and identically distributed, but the parameters of the distribution (μ or σ^2) are uncertain, or if the $\eta(t)$ parameter declines, rather than remains constant (Gollier and Hammitt, 2014).[37]

A common modification to the Ramsey rule is to add a small risk premium to the ρ term to account for catastrophic events, such as nuclear wars or natural

---

[35] This view reflects the fact that the Ramsey rule can be derived as a first-order condition from an economic growth model.

[36] Drupp et al. (2018) present the results of an expert survey that includes opinions about the appropriate normative/positive balance in setting the SDR.

[37] Risk premia can also be added to the Ramsey rule, to account for the effect of systematic project risks. See Gollier (2013, chapter 12) and Groom et al. (2022) for this and other Ramsey rule extensions.

disasters, that pose an existential risk to humanity. Dietz and Stern (2008) suggest a risk premium of 0.1 percent, representing a 1 in 1,000 annual risk. The British Government adds a 1 percent risk premium to the Ramsey discount rate to cover a combination of catastrophic risk and systematic risk arising from the covariance of project returns and economic growth.

The Ramsey rule has also been extended to account for expected temporal trends in the relative value of environmental services and produced consumption goods. In this context, environmental services and produced consumption goods enter utility, and a modified CDR is derived with the environmental services taken as a parameter in the optimization (Gollier and Hammitt, 2014). Given standard assumptions about the functional form of utility, the net-return on savings is $r - p$, where p is the rate at which the value of the environment services changes relative to consumption (Hoel and Sterner, 2007). This lowers the effective discount rate for $p > 0$.

It is commonly assumed that the growth rate of produced consumption goods is higher than environmental services (which may be declining with economic growth). Technical progress extends the supply of produced consumption goods while environmental services are relatively inelastic. It is also assumed that the elasticity of substitution between environmental services and private consumption goods is relatively low, implying that the value of environmental services is increasing over time as they become relatively scarcer.[38] Making these assumptions, and assuming the relatively high initial discount rate used in the DICE model (5.2 percent), Sterner and Persson (2008) show that optimal carbon emissions trajectories are lower beyond about 2080 than those found in the Stern report using a lower initial discount rate (3.4 percent). In other words, relative price changes have a significant impact on the effective discount rate.[39]

An "environmental discount rate" can also be derived with environmental services treated as the choice variable and consumption taken as a parameter (Gollier and Hammitt, 2014). If there is no substitutability between environmental services and consumption, "dual discount rates" for environmental services and for consumption become necessary (Weikard and Zhu, 2005).

The standard Ramsey discount rate is consistent with the Ramsey/Cass-Koopmans (RCK) economic growth model. The economic growth literature also includes models that treat growth as endogenous, and models that add human capital and environmental resources to production and/or utility

---

[38] This argument was originally made in Krutilla (1967).

[39] The same result can be achieved by forecasting relative price movements, and discounting at the standard consumption rate (Groom et al. 2022).

functions, among other modifications (e.g., Acemoglu et al., 2012; Dietz and Venmans, 2019; Krutilla and Reuveny 2002, 2004, 2006; Xepapadeas, 2005). The first order conditions from these models yield differential equations for consumption growth that imply consumption rates of discount. As an example, adding "nature capital" the utility function of a standard RCK model yields an augmented model in which increasing consumption in the present reduces future utility through two channels (Krutilla and Reuveny, 2002). First, as in the standard Ramsey framework, future consumption of the produced consumption good declines with lower investment. Second, environmental amenities decline with less nature capital regenerated, lowering welfare through the direct utility channel. These dual impacts are reflected in a modified Ramsey rule: $r = \rho + \eta g - \frac{V_s}{U_c}$. The added term, $\frac{V_s}{U_c}$, is the marginal rate of substitution of the environmental amenity for consumption. Because $\frac{V_s}{U_c} > 0$, the effect of the resource-generated amenity is to lower the Ramsey discount rate; thus, the steady state exhibits a higher level of (nature) capital and a lower level of consumption than in the standard Ramsey model. In contrast to the literature on relative price changes, this result obtains when resources and consumption are perfectly substitutable (the condition assumed in this stylized model), and whatever the change in the growth rates of consumption and natural resources (which are identical in this model along a balanced growth path, giving $\frac{V_s}{U_c}$ as a constant). This is just one example from a large economic growth literature of how the economic context can matter for structuring the Ramsey discount rate.

5.4 The Social Opportunity Cost of Capital

5.4.1 The SOC and Weighted Cost-of-Capital Method

The SOC, or its weighted cost-of-capital extension, is recommended by Burgess and Zerbe (2011), Harberger and Jenkins (2015), and Harrison (2010) among others. The real, before-tax rate of return on capital is generally taken to represent the SOC. It is higher than a CDR derived from the bond market by the sum of risk premia, capital taxes, and taxes on interest paid to savers. The United States and Canada recommends SOC rates of 7 percent and 8 percent in their regulatory guidance. Latin American countries commonly use the SOC method as well. Rates for OECD members in the region range from 6 percent (Chile) to 10 percent (Mexico). See Groom et al. (2022).

The national income accounts are commonly used to derive a rate of return on reproducible capital. The process involves dividing income from reproducible capital by the existing level of capital stock.[40] The rate provides an average

---

[40] See Burgess and Zerbe (2011), CEA (2017), Harberger and Jenkins (2015), and Harrison (2010) for the implementation details.

across all sectors in the economy and classes of reproducible capital and embodies an average risk premium. Proponents believe that an economy-wide average is the relevant measure for the capital opportunity costs associated with public policies. According to Harberger and Jenkins (2015), this rate provides a reasonable "rule of thumb."

In the general case, raising public finance is assumed to displace private investment and consumption, and to attract funds from abroad. To capture these effects, a weighted opportunity cost of capital, R, can be formulated as $R = \alpha 1 SOC + \alpha 2 CDR + \alpha 3 F$, where the alpha parameters are the funding shares from the different sources ($\alpha 1 + \alpha 2 + \alpha 3 = 1$) and F is the return earned on foreign funds after tax (Burgess and Zerbe, 2011). Variation in taxes throughout the OECD imply different after-tax returns on foreign investments.

Although the global capital market is integrated, Burgess and Zerbe (2011) argue that the net supply of foreign funds is not infinitely elastic. When domestic interest rates rise, foreign direct investment is squeezed out, partially offsetting the induced increase in external portfolio investment. These combined effects can be captured in a "saving retention coefficient," which have been estimated for all OECD countries (see Burgess and Zerbe, 2011).

Foreign borrowing is often ignored in the United States. In this case, proponents of the SOC argue that investment is more interest rate-sensitive than consumer savings, so that displaced capital investment comprises the bulk of the weight in the weighted SOC (Harrison, 2010; Harberger and Jenkins, 2015). However, interest rate responsiveness declines in models incorporating real options (see Dixit et al., 1994). Given the uncertainty about weights, Circular A-4 recommends using the CDR and the SOC in bounding sensitivity analyses.

Critics point out that using the CDR and SOC in bounding sensitivity analysis or in a weighted capital combination mixes discount rates with different risk profiles, that is, the CDR is a riskless rate, while the SOC contains a risk premium. Basing the discount on an average economy rate of return also ignores regulation-specific risks. Additionally, because IAMs use consumption as the numeraire, the CDR is the appropriate rate for estimating the SCC.[41]

5.4.2 Shadow Price of Capital

The "shadow price of capital" can give the same result as the weighted cost-of-capital method, under some conditions.[42] To illustrate, consider a simple two-period model in which a dollar is invested in an initial period

---

[41] We are indebted to two reviewers for these points.

[42] The literature on the shadow price of capital assumes a closed economy.

yielding a single consumption benefit, B, in the following period. The social cost of a unit of investment in the initial period can be converted into a consumption numeraire using $\theta_o = a\nu + (1 - a)$, where θ_o is the shadow price of capital (in present value units of consumption); α and $(1 - \alpha)$ are the shares of investment and consumption diverted by a public policy, and $\nu \equiv \frac{1+r}{1+r_c}$ gives the present value, from the consumer perspective, of the rate of return on capital (using r to denote the SOC and r_c to denote the CDR for notational convenience).[43] Given these definitions, the net present value (NPV) of a dollar of investment using the consumption numeraire is $NPV = -\theta_o + \frac{B}{1+r_c}$. Dividing through by θ_o and simplifying gives the NPV in dollars terms:

$$\frac{NPV}{\theta_o} = -1 + \frac{B}{\alpha(1 + r) + (1 - \alpha)(1 + r_c)}.$$

The right-hand side gives the weighted cost-of-capital method. Li and Pizer (2021) show that the consistency of the shadow price of capital method and the weighted cost-of-capital discount rate also holds when future consumption benefits are in the form of an annuity.

In the more general case, the time horizon is variable, future benefits are not in the form of an annuity, and not all benefits are consumed. Li and Pizer (2021) derive a general formula encompassing these conditions:

$$SDR = (1 + r_c)\left(\frac{\theta_o}{\theta_t}\right)^{\frac{1}{t}} - 1.$$

The new element, θ_t, is the shadow value of benefits in period t given that some fraction of the benefits in each period are reinvested. When $\theta_o = \theta_t$, the *SDR* goes to r_c (the *CDR*). Li and Pizer (2021) explore a range of other plausible values for $\frac{\theta_o}{\theta_t}$. When the time horizon is short, for example, $t < 10$, the ratio $\frac{\theta_o}{\theta_t}$ dominates the result, but as the time horizon increases, the ratio becomes less significant. For a fifty-year horizon under best estimates for parameter values and a 3 percent CDR, the range of possible SDRs falls to between 2.3 percent and 3.8 percent (Li and Pizer, 2021). As $t \to \infty$, $\left(\frac{\theta_o}{\theta_t}\right)^t \to 1$, and SDR converges to the consumption rate of discount.

Critics argue that the shadow price of capital approach is not practical to implement (Harrison, 2010), and that exogenous reinvestment rates are inconsistent with savings behavior (Burgess and Zerbe, 2011). Li and Pizer (2021) address the later point assuming that the underlying dynamic system is in a steady state, giving constant consumption and savings rates, and derive the discount rate using a Ramsey model.

---

[43] This example is taken from Li and Pizer (2021).

5.5 On-Budget versus Off-Budget Financing

The positive discounting literature assumes that government budgets finance projects, and the financing is sourced from the capital market.[44] As noted in Section 5.4, the associated financing opportunity costs are additional consumer savings, displaced investments, and borrowing from foreign sources. This paradigm reflects the origins of BCA in infrastructure evaluation. For several reasons, the context for regulatory evaluation is quite different. As noted in Section 3, output adjustments offer one margin for regulatory compliance. For polluters, reducing output provides *operational cost savings,* rather than additional capital costs. The opportunity costs associated with output reductions – foregone consumption – are entirely borne by consumers. On the inframarginal output range, polluters may bear some of the costs. But except for the case of technology standards, polluters have considerable flexibility for input adjustments that do not require capital. An example is the compliance achieved by US utility plants from fuel-switching to national gas from 2005 to 2015, rather than installing pollution controls. Overall, the capital cost share in total social costs is likely to be significantly lower for regulations than for infrastructure projects.

The SDR using the opportunity cost approach should reflect the impact of government interventions on the marginal trade-off of current for future consumption in the entire economy – an inherently GE concept. In this context, the incidence of regulatory compliance costs is relevant. In GE models using constant returns to scale production technology, all compliance costs are borne by consumers. Specifications which allow upward sloping supply in some sectors allow pass-through rates of less than 100 percent, consistent with the literature on regulatory pass-through. Whatever the degree of pass-through, consumer prices in CGE regulatory cost models increase in response to regulations, affecting real wages and labor supply (see Section 3).

A relevant question is how GE adjustments affect consumer behavior in the credit markets they use. This question has not been explored in the discounting literature. If consumers use of credit markets is impacted by regulation, the opportunity costs are likely to be high. Credit rationing is pervasive in the economy (Stern et al., 2022). Several studies have documented high marginal rates of consumer time preference consistent with credit rationing. For example, the choices of US military personnel about compensation packages offered as part of downsizing program revealed implicit nominal discount rates between 10 percent and 54 percent (Warner and Pleeter, 2001). A field study in Denmark showed a mean nominal rate of 28 percent (Harrison et al., 2002).

---

[44] In the case of tax financed projects, Burgess and Zerbe (2011) argue that the capital market provides the relevant opportunity cost, because paying down debt is always a policy option.

An implicit nominal discount rate of 77 percent and a mean required payback period of 3.7 years were estimated in a revealed preference study of energy investment behavior in Greece (Damigos et al., 2021). Demographic characteristics, such as income and education, affected these estimates, as well as the size of investment costs (Damigos et al., 2021).

RIAs of energy efficiency regulations in the United States have had to confront the disparity between consumer behavior and the economic parameters assumed in the analysis. RIAs commonly show that the market value of energy savings is high enough to pay off private costs, using standard assumptions about SDRs and other economic parameters. Why markets do not independently offer these technologies is a puzzle known as the "energy efficiency gap" or "energy efficiency paradox" (see Gillingham and Palmer (2014) and Helfand and Dorsey-Palmateer (2015)). Consumer discount rates that are higher than the assumed SDRs is one possible reason for this discrepancy. Bounded rationality and low levels of financial literacy are also possible causes.

The distinctive incidence of regulations, and the possible relevance of GE effects for discount rates in regulatory evaluation, have not been addressed in the discounting literature. Exploring this topic would be a worthy objective for future research.

5.6 Dichotomizing Efficiency and Intergenerational Equity

Using two policy instruments to promote two policy objectives, if the choice of instruments is unconstrained, is a basic optimization principle. Using intergenerational wealth transfers to address intergenerational equity, while undertaking high yield investments to promote economic efficiency, is an application of this principle. Suppose the CDR is 2 percent and the SOC is 8 percent. A $1,000 energy investment yielding a single consumption benefit at 2 percent would give the equivalent of $7,389 in 100 years. However, only $2.48 invested in a sovereign wealth fund yielding 8 percent would give the same result.[45] Or investing $1,000 at 8 percent would give $2,980,942 in 100 years. Pursuing a Pareto improving strategy that provides these gains is the most economically efficient way to address intergenerational concerns (see Burgess and Zerbe (2011), Harrison (2010), Lind (1995), Weisbach and Sunstein (2008), and Weyant (2008)).[46]

An intuitive way to implement this principle is for the current generation to decide upon the magnitude of the intergenerational transfer; for example, the

---

[45] Sovereign wealth funds earn income from diversified portfolios that include foreign equities. Returns earned abroad may be subject to foreign income taxes – or be exempt as in the United States. This example abstracts from tax considerations.

[46] Debt management can also be used to effect intergenerational transfers, for example, accelerating debt retirement to lower future-generation tax liabilities. See Liu et al. (2021).

size of the endowment for a sovereign wealth fund. Conditional on this decision, all generations would support investments from the fund that maximize future returns (Kaplow, 2006). Suppose that the fund's long-run rate of return is expected to be z percent. The fund could be used to finance projects impacting future generations with social returns greater than z percent, or the fund could be allowed to grow at z percent. This context is completely analogous to capital budgeting, with z percent the discount rate for prioritizing projects having long-lasting effects.

This concept seems appealing for the public financing of long-lasting infra-structure, and R&D in basic sciences, early-stage energy development, biotech-nology, computer and information systems, and the like. It seems less appealing for addressing environmental issues having uncertain but enduring and irrevers-ible effects – such as the accumulation of atmospheric carbon stocks. In this case, transfers to future generations, either as compensation, or to finance adaptations, might be less than originally assumed to be necessary to meet intergenerational obligations. Moreover, the low substitutability between produced goods and environmental services could render money compensations relatively ineffective.

A better approach is to adopt a budget limitation based on an environmental performance metric, rather than a money metric. Of course, this is exactly the approach of target-consistent carbon pricing. As noted in the previous section, the objective of target-consistent carbon pricing is to direct investments to projects yielding the lowest net costs, consistent with a stipulated emissions trajectory. Although the discounting literature has discussed a SCC-compatible discounting approach (Newell et al., 2022), the discounting implications of the target-consistent carbon pricing method have not been considered, to our knowledge. It is intuitive that the appropriate discount rate is closer to the long-term yield on a sovereign wealth fund than a CDR; the latter will not be stringent enough to sort out more from less efficient projects. Moreover, a lower rate motivated by intergenerational equity concerns is not apt in this context, given that intergener-ational concerns are addressed ex ante when the emissions target is established. The discounting implications of the target-consistent carbon pricing deserve additional research, in view of the paucity of academic literature on this subject.

6 Distributional Effects

6.1 Introduction

AEC regulations impose uncompensated losses on private actors and offer a mix of market and nonmarket benefits to large populations. The beneficiaries are not necessarily the individuals who bear the costs. This profile makes the distributional effects of regulations both policy relevant and difficult to assess.

Distributional impacts can be categorized along different dimensions, including factor income and employment; position in the market as a producer or consumer; business size, or entry date into the market; jurisdictional level; regional demarcation, or some combination. Benefit-cost analysis guidance documents recognize the importance of distributional effects, and distributional concerns are reflected in policy designs that favor some constituencies (small business, incumbent polluters) over others. However, owing to complexity of the distributional pattern for AEC regulations, distributional assessments in RIAs are often relatively limited. The most common practice is to identify impacts by identifiable stakeholder groups, like small business or labor in regulated industries, when information is available.

AEC regulations are sometimes perceived as having regressive effects on worker incomes and employment. Lower income individuals are disproportionately employed in polluting industries and spend a larger share of income on energy-intensive goods, like electricity and fuel. However, the literature suggests a more nuanced picture. The impacts of regulations on lower income individuals depend on the type of regulation, the structure of the economy, regional environmental effects and demographic patterns, and institutional characteristics, such as the nature of the tax and transfer system. These factors are likely to empirically vary by specific regulatory and economic context.

CGE models can provide income class-disaggregated surplus measures for policy change that embody all welfare channels represented in the model. The income spectrum is typically stratified into quintiles or deciles; however, Rauch et al., (2011) develop a CGE model that disaggregates effects on individual households. Welfare effects can also be demarcated by countries or regions within a common economic area, such as the EU (Mayeres and Van Regemorter, 2008)

The distributional literature commonly focuses on one or more aspects of the total welfare effect of a regulation, to better understand the components. This practice drives the structure of this section. Following the expositional format in Fullerton (2011), we start with an assessment of the burden of regulations on producers and production factors. The next topic is the impacts of regulations on consumers. We then consider how the allocation of pollution rents affects distributional impacts. Last, we review the distribution of the health and environmental benefits that AEC regulations provide.

6.2 The Burden of Regulations on the Supply Side

AEC regulations have two sorts of effects on workers, capital owners, and other production factors. First, if the regulation affects relative input prices broadly in the economy, the earnings of factors that remain employed will change. The net-effect depends on the share of income received from different sources and the impact of the regulation on their returns. Second, the incentive effect of AEC regulations will alter the allocation of inputs in the economy, giving rise to both efficiency costs and distributional effects. As discussed in Section 3, economic structure and regulatory design influence the burden of the regulation on the supply and demand sides, driving the extent of these changes.

The relative burden of government interventions on labor and capital is widely studied. The classic research on corporate tax incidence by Harberger (1962) shows that results are extremely sensitive to the parameterizations of utility and production functions. These results carry over in extensions that add emissions into the production function and analyze the burdens of an emissions tax (Fullerton and Heutel, 2007) and a standard limiting emissions per unit of output (Fullerton and Heutel, 2010). Whether emissions restrictions relatively burden capital or labor more heavily is quite ambiguous in these models.

Harberger-type models represent the boundary case where labor and capital are in fixed supply. Another limiting case is when supply of capital is freely mobile at a fixed world rate of return. In this situation, the burden of an environmental tax falls exclusively on labor and consumers (Fullerton and Muehlegger, 2019).

Production factors in these models are fully employed in equilibrium, and adjustment costs are not fully represented. Unemployment and adjustment costs are often politically salient. Concerns about asset-specific capital losses that arose in the United States in the era of utility restructuring have again resurfaced in the context of climate regulations, which are likely to accelerate the retirements of fossil-fuel plants (Caldecott, 2018). Workers whose skills are closely tied to their current use or location have limited adjustment flexibility and may become involuntarily unemployed. To the extent that sector-specific labor unemployment is long-lasting, the personal and societal costs are well established (Bartik, 2015; Haveman and Weimer, 2015). If such employment effects can be accurately measured and attributed to AEC regulation, the social costs are relevant for both the distributional and efficiency analysis.

Labor that is not occupation or sector-specific can relocate at a relatively low transition cost without a significant change in earnings. Even in this case, however, welfare losses are likely. An equilibrium sorting model by Kuminoff et al. (2015) demonstrates why. In this model, individuals make simultaneous choices about employment and living locations. Changing locations affects employment possibilities and income, but also other attributes, such as commuting distances, housing choices, and community characteristics. Given that these other attributes affect welfare, economic estimates of involuntary relocations based on earnings differences alone can understate welfare losses.

Partial equilibrium models are sometimes used to assess the net employment impact of environmental regulation on regulated sectors. The effects on sectoral output prices are incorporated into these models, but factor prices and other commodity prices are typically held constant. Using this approach, Belova et al. (2015) show that three factors influence the employment impact of a regulation. First, holding labor per unit of output constant, labor usage will decline from the output substitution effect discussed in Section 3. Secondly, and again holding labor intensity constant, labor usage will increase as a function of the cost increase the regulation brings about. Third, the regulation can change labor intensity, increasing or decreasing the share of labor in total cost. With the first two factors having opposite impacts on employment, and the third directionally ambiguous – depending on whether labor is a substitute or complement with the regulated input – a regulation's overall effect on sectoral employment is ambiguous.

The employment effect of regulations economy-wide has been studied in CGE models that incorporate labor market processes with equilibrium unemployment. Union bargaining is one explanation for the persistence of involuntary unemployment. Union bargaining models have been used to explain labor market behavior in Europe, where unions are relatively influential. A "right-to-manage" model is an example. In this framework, trade unions and employer representatives negotiate over a wage rate. After the wage is determined, firms choose the employment level that maximize profits (Koskela, 2001).

The employment effects of "green tax reforms" have been studied in analytical GE models that incorporate a union bargaining process. The tax reform consists of shifting taxes from labor to dirty polluting goods or energy inputs while maintaining budget balance. The employment effect of tax shifting among consumption goods is found to be ambiguous (Koskela and Schob, 1999). Institutional characteristics, such as whether unemployment benefits are indexed to the price level, affects the results. Shifting taxes from labor to energy can increase the equilibrium employment level if labor is substitutable enough with energy in production (Koskela et al., 1998).

Search-friction models are another way to model equilibrium unemployment (Hafstead and Williams (2020)). In this setup, firms determine the supply of vacancies and incur a cost to post vacancy announcements. Job searching imposes transactions costs on prospective workers. The employment success rate is a function of the number of job searches and vacancies, with the probability of securing employment less than one. Labor market frictions create a gap between the marginal product of labor and a jobseekers' time opportunity costs. Once a job is located, bargaining over the wage share of the surplus – often modeled using a Nash assumption– is necessary before the employment process is finalized.[47]

An analytical model by Bovenberg and van der Ploeg (1998) incorporate a search-friction labor market to study the effect of a revenue-neutral shift from labor to energy taxes. This model represents both informal and formal sectors. Tax shifting has ambiguous effects on the equilibrium employment level, depending on economic factors (whether income in the informal sector is linked to productivity in the formal sector) and institutional factors (how unemployment benefits are indexed).

Hafstead and Williams (2020) study the sectoral and economy-wide employment impacts of environmental policies in a CGE model with a search-friction type labor market. As is common in CGE models, this model captures the employment effects of upstream and downstream linkages, and the effects of consumer demand shifts from changes in product prices. The search-friction labor market adds an additional adjustment channel, involving the matching process between job seekers and prospective employers and the bargaining process over wages. The study considers three types of environmental policies. The first is a sector-specific regulation, modeled as an input cost shock, that targets durable manufacturing. This is taken to represent a technology-based standard. The second is a tradable performance standard implemented in the utility sector that limits CO_2 emissions per megawatt hour generated over the entire industry. The final policy is an economy-wide carbon tax. In all cases, labor taxes are adjusted to maintain budget balance. The policies differ in magnitude (which is not the principal focus of the study). The results are presented for the employment effect in the regulated sectors, the sectors that contract from the regulation ("negative spillover sectors"), those that expand ("positive spillover sectors"), and the sum for the total economy (see Table 1). In all cases, the employment effect in the regulated sector provides a biased picture of the economy-wide effect, and labor reallocations among sectors are significant. A durable manufacturing regulation decreases net employment in the regulated sector, owing to an output substitution effect that reduces labor demand. The net of spillovers in other sectors is to increase economy-wide losses further (see Table 1). In contrast, the power-sector performance standard increases net employment in the regulated sector. Labor is substituted for energy and the rate-based structure of the standard affords an implicit output subsidy that helps to maintain employment. However, the net of spillover effects in other sectors leads to a negative economy-wide employment impact. The carbon tax has a negative employment impact on energy industries, but the

---

[47] This model was pioneered by Pissarides (2000).

Table 1 Employment effects of environmental regulation
(percent of total employment)

	Regulated sectors (%)	Negative spillover sectors (%)	Positive spillover sectors (%)	All sectors (%)
Durable manufacturing regulation	−0.019	−0.037	0.02	−0.036
Power-sector performance standard	0.041	−0.049	0.002	−0.006
Economy-wide carbon tax (with labor tax cuts)	−0.032	−0.343	0.396	0.021

Source: Adapted from Hafstead and Williams (2020).

net of spillover effects is to increase employment economy-wide, with the revenue recycling mechanism playing a role in this outcome (Hafstead and Williams, 2020). The nuances of this distributional picture suggest the value of disaggregating the incidence of employment impacts beyond the regulated market.

6.3 The Burden of Regulations on Consumers

Some of the cost of regulations is likely to be passed on to consumers. The burden is purely distributional for inframarginal units of consumption, while conventionally efficiency and adjustment costs arise on the consumption foregone. In either case, the regulation most significantly burdens consumers having preregulation expenditures weighted relatively heavily in goods that increase in price, such as electricity or fuel. A common question is whether this burden falls more heavily on low-income consumers than those of other income classes.

Flues and Thomas (2015) review consumer expenditure data in OECD countries to assess the burden of energy taxes on different income classes and types of households. As is typical of expenditure-based simulation studies, the study considers the purely distributional effect on inframarginal units of consumption as the price of energy rises. The study finds that the burden of energy taxes varies by the type of the fuel. Comparing these burdens against total consumer expenditures, electricity taxes among OECD countries are generally regressive. Expenditure share on electricity declines as total consumption expenditures increase. Taxes on heating fuels are shown to be mildly regressive, while taxes on transportation fuels are progressive on a 21-country average but vary significantly by country. For example, transportation fuel taxes are progressive in countries with lower per capita GDPs but are proportional or mildly regressive in countries with higher per capita GDPs (Flues and Thomas, 2015). The result is attributable to lower automobile usage among lower income households in poorer countries. These results are generally consistent with a review by Pizer and Sexton (2019), based on similar methodology.

In another study, Cronin et al. (2019) use expenditure data to show that a carbon tax imposed in the United States is somewhat progressive. While the share of carbon emissions as a fraction of consumer expenditure is relatively constant across income classes, lower income consumers receive a larger fraction of their income as transfer payments. These payments are indexed to the price level, so transfer payments increase when a carbon tax is imposed and prices increase.

Davis and Knittle (2019) study the burden of Corporate Average Fuel Economy standards in the United States. These standards provide an implicit subsidy to smaller fuel-efficient cars and an implicit tax on larger cars. Because higher income families buy a relatively larger share of new cars, the standards are mildly progressive when only new vehicle sales are considered. However, the standard also has the effect of shifting some demand to the used car market, thereby raising used car prices. Including the used car market makes the standards mildly regressive, given that low-income consumers disproportionately buy used cars. In either case, the effects are not large compared to average annual household income.

Levinson (2019) compares the distributional properties of energy efficiency regulations versus emissions taxes. Consumers pay for efficiency in the purchase price of appliances with differing energy efficiency ratings, and for the usage level through expenditures on energy to operate the appliances. Lower income consumers ordinarily buy older less efficient appliances and run them less than higher income consumers. This behavior translates into a lower level of energy consumption in lower income households. An efficiency regulation forces consumers to buy efficiency. This is relatively less burdensome for richer households who are already purchasing energy efficient appliances. An energy tax burdens both lower and higher income households. But rich households pay more owing to their higher energy consumption levels. Given these differing effects, it turns out that both appliance efficiency standards and energy taxes are regressive, but energy taxes are less regressive than efficiency standards.

Horizontal distributional effects are also increasingly studied in the literature. Heating and cooling loads, modal transportation choices, commuting patterns and travel distances, and the composition and price of energy sources differ within and across regions. These heterogeneities introduce differences in end-use energy loads, holding incomes constant. Household characteristics, including family size and age, also affect energy consumption. In the United States and the United Kingdom, these factors cause variation in energy consumption within income classes that can equal or exceed variation across them, depending on the energy source (Pizer and Sexton, 2019). For the bottom 40 percent of the consumption distribution, Cronin et al. (2019) find that the burden of a carbon tax varies more widely among consumers within income classes than between the averages for the lowest and highest deciles. In a static computable GE model that represents all channels affecting distributional burdens, the burden of a $20 carbon tax also varies significantly within income deciles (Rauch et al., 2011).

6.4 The Distribution of Pollution Rents

Inframarginal rents on regulated pollution are significantly larger than abatement costs unless the level of regulation is stringent. The magnitude and political salience of these rents, particularly for policies restricting carbon emissions, raise important distributional issues.

One option is to distribute some rents to polluters to compensate (or partially compensate) for abatement costs. When abatement costs can be significantly passed onto consumers, a relatively small share of pollution rents is needed for compensation. A CGE study by Bovenberg and Goulder (2002) of a $25/ton carbon tax imposed on coal, oil, and natural gas suppliers showed that only 4.3 percent of rents earned from the coal industry and 15 percent from oil and natural gas producers were needed for complete compensation.

Carbon rents can also be used to defray consumer burdens. Rebating revenues lump sum across income can make carbon taxes progress (Rauch et al., 2011). However, Cronin et al. (2019) show that heterogeneities in household characteristics within income classes complicate the compensation of low-income consumers. The institutional structure of the tax and transfer system does not allow the differentiation of transfer schemes to fully reflect household heterogeneities.

A basic constraint is that there are not enough carbon rents to compensate all claimants (Dinan and Holtz-Eakin, 2003). Under these conditions, a large rent-seeking literature shows that the resource costs associated with the rent-seeking activities can attenuate or fully the dissipate rents, for example, Pérez-Castrillo and Verdier (1992). An extension to market-based environmental policies demonstrates significant rent-seeking costs (MacKenzie and Ohndorf, 2012). Game-theoretic models of political competition show that the costs associated with policy contestation can exceed abatement costs (Krutilla and Alexeev, 2012, 2014).

The key intuition is that conventional efficiency costs are manifest at the margins, while policy-related transaction costs are incentivized over the entire inframarginal and marginal ranges of the regulated activity (Krutilla and Krause, 2011).

Expanding the menu of policy options could reduce the costs of rent-seeking and political transaction costs. One option is to pair carbon taxes or auctioned tradable permit systems with deregulatory initiatives. Price-based instruments are a substitute for the prescriptive regulations that industries find burdensome. Hence, the option of transitioning from the existing regulatory system to a price-based system would open-up a channel for policy reform. Additionally, the way carbon rents are used should be considered within the context of the full menu of fiscal policy options. It is economically inefficient to treat the allocation of pollution rents as the only policy instrument for achieving distributional objectives, and risks incentivizing high policy transaction costs.

6.5 The Distribution of Benefits

Benefits associated with AEC regulations include energy savings and the value of reducing emissions. The PE distribution of these benefits is considered in this subsection.

Energy savings arise from the use of more efficient consumer appliances or vehicles, or from process adjustments and/or new technology in the commercial or industrial sectors. In the former case, the benefits of energy savings fall on consumers. The benefits of commercial or industrial energy savings are partially borne on the supply side, and partially passed on to consumers as lower prices and/or greater consumption.

Reducing air pollution exposures produces the variety of benefits indicated in Figure 1, Section 4. The benefits of reducing health care costs falls on some combination of health insurers (private and public), health care providers, and consumers, depending on the institutional structure of health insurance systems. The value of improving productivity in renewable resource sectors is distributed among suppliers and consumers of resource-derived products. Increasing labor productivity will be distributed as combination of higher profits for employers and higher wages for workers; consumers experience the benefits of any increases in leisure time. The productivity effects from better conditioned commercial building structures or materials will be shared between the supply and demand sides of the market. The increased value of residential property, and the benefits of reducing haze and improving visibility, are borne by consumers.

Two factors influence the distribution of morbidity and mortality benefits associated with improving air quality. First, regulations reduce exposure risks nonuniformly among regions. Secondly, for a given exposure reduction, marginal valuations vary among individuals (Hsiang et al., 2019). One reason marginal valuations are likely to differ across populations is that health or environmental damage associated with air pollution are nonlinear in the level of exposures. If damage functions are convex, marginal damage reductions will decline as air quality improves, translating into declining marginal valuations – all else constant. The standard assumption of diminishing marginal utility independently predicts the same relationship. These factors imply that baseline exposures will influence the marginal value of exposure reductions, and that individuals facing different exposures will be located on different parts of marginal damage functions.

Socio-demographic heterogeneities also give rise to different marginal valuations, holding exposure risk reductions constant (Hsiang et al., 2019). Population characteristics, such as age, health status, and ethnicity, are likely to influence the health effects of air pollution, for example, Chay and Greenstone (2003). Preference parameters vary among individuals, for example, parents may have relatively strong preferences for better air quality out of concern for their children (Grainger, 2012). Relatively health-conscious consumers are more likely to take averting actions, like wearing face masks, staying indoors on a polluted day, or purchasing air conditions or filtration equipment – all else constant. These actions affect valuations and should be incorporated into WTP estimates (Deschenes et al., 2017). The effect of income is another source of variability. Higher income individuals should have relatively high marginal valuations – again holding all else constant – if air quality is a normal good.

Generalizing about the distributional impacts of these factors is challenging. For example, the evidence suggests that lower income populations and ethnic minorities experience higher exposure risks than other demographics (Jbaily et al., 2022; Tessum et al., 2021; Thind et al., 2019). All else constant, this would position lower income individuals on higher points on the marginal damage functions. But lower income individuals also are likely to have lower WTPs, making the combined effect ambiguous.[48]

It is hard to empirically sort out these effects, and differences in marginal valuations are ignored in RIA.[49] One concentration-response (C-R) coefficient is used to represent a specific health effect of a particular pollutant – for example, the effect of PM2.5 on all-cause mortality – without differentiation for population characteristics (Levy, 2021). Population-averaged unit values, such as the VSL, are taken to represent marginal values. The consequence is that

---

[48] See Banzhaf and Timmins (2019) on the environmental justice issues associated with income disparities.

[49] Population heterogeneities are likely to be endogenous or correlated with omitted variables (Hsiang et al., 2019).

reducing exposure risks nonuniformly is the only channel through which distributional effects on the benefit side can be differentiated in current RIA practice.[50] In fact, some evidence suggests that regulations do reduce exposure risks nonuniformly. Bento et al. (2015) found that enforcement of the 1990 Clean Air Act amendments targeted polluters in areas closest to pollution monitors in nonattainment regions. These areas have relatively large populations of lower income homeowners.

The incidence of benefits can be realized as changes in property valuations – the basis for the large benefit valuation literature using hedonic models. Measuring changes in property values, Bento et al. (2015) found that the annual benefits of PM10 reductions from the 1990 Clean Air Act amendments are about twice as high as a fraction of annual income for lowest quintile of homeowners than for the highest, owing to the location of low-income homeowners in polluted areas, and the larger impact of regulation in these areas. For rental properties, the incidence of capitalized values is distributed between renters and landlords. A study by Grainger (2012) found that about half of the capitalized value of local air quality improvements was captured in higher rental rates. Bento et al. (2015) found that rental rates were not significantly affected by changes in air pollution except for units located relatively close to air pollution monitors.

The distribution of economic damage from global climate damage is a function of the magnitude of physical climate effects and their marginal valuation (Hsiang et al., 2019). Local and regional climate effects, such as precipitation patterns, hydrological conditions, storm frequency and intensity, are heterogenous across regions. Damage functions are likely to be nonlinear and socioeconomic conditions vary widely for different populations. In a review of the literature, Hsiang et al. (2019) conclude that physical climate effects are not necessarily greater for lower income populations, but that marginal damage are likely to be higher owing to demographic heterogeneities and nonlinearities in damage functions (Hsiang et al., 2019). In the literature on natural disasters, low-income populations are found to be particularly vulnerable to climate change, for example, Hallegatte et al. (2020).

7 Uncertainty Evaluation

7.1 Introduction

The economic evaluation of AEC regulations confronts numerous uncertainties that arise in the following areas: (1) the forecast of economic conditions, energy usage, and emissions trajectories in the counterfactual state of the world without

---

[50] RIA practice is subject to evolving information and political judgements, so this may change in the future.

the regulation; (2) the effect of the regulatory intervention on energy usage and emissions trajectories; (3) the effect of changes in emissions trajectories on ambient concentrations; (4) the effects of ambient concentrations on exposures, health, and environmental damages; and (5) the valuation of damages. The costs associated the regulatory intervention are also uncertain, as noted in Section 3. Credibly addressing these uncertainties poses an analytical challenge.

In an ideal world, uncertainties would be identified and addressed at every stage of regulatory development and assessment. At the earliest stages of regulatory design, an evaluation would be made of modifications of the structure of the regulation or additional information that reduces uncertainties. At the analysis stage, regulatory alternatives would be systematically compared to assess how uncertainties affect the NPV comparison. At the reporting stage, the regulatory BCA would indicate the level of confidence about the results of the economic analysis, with transparency about the mechanisms that cause the uncertainties. In practice, the uncertainty analysis in RIAs can significantly depart from this ideal.

This section starts with a taxonomy of the levels of uncertainty that can arise in the BCA of AEC regulations. Uncertainty evaluation methods are then considered.

7.2 Uncertainty Levels

How to taxonomize uncertainty is the subject of a large decision-science literature. The classical work by Knight (1921) defines "risk" as the case that parameter values have known outcomes with known probabilities; "uncertainty" as the case that outcomes are known but their probabilities are unknown, and "ignorance" as the situation when even possible outcomes are unknown. Not surprisingly, researchers have proposed numerous additional taxonomies in the more than 100 years following Knight's seminal work.[51] Recent literature parses the distinctions along the uncertainty-to-ignorance part of Knight's spectrum, using such terminology as "deep" or "fundamental" uncertainty. Walker et al. (2013) define "Level 4" uncertainty as the context where the probability of outcomes cannot be quantitatively specified but can still be ranked according to their likelihood, while "Level 5" uncertainty denotes more fundamental uncertainty approximating "ignorance" in Knight's definition. Lempert et al. (2013) define fundamental uncertainty as a situation where "the parties to a decision cannot agree upon (1) the appropriate models to describe interactions among system variables, (2) the probability distributions to represent uncertainty about key parameters in the models, and/or (3) how to

---

[51] See Krupnick et al. (2006) for a review.

value the desirability of alternative outcomes." For our purposes, "less fundamental uncertainty" is defined as the situation that models are reasonably well-
accepted, and parameter values are locally uncertain within "reasonably small
ranges," while "more fundamental uncertainty" is the case that researchers have
alternative views and significant disagreements about the structure of models
and the value of parameters. We now turn to methods that can be used to address
"less fundamental uncertainty," before considering decision-science
approaches that are relevant for incorporating "more fundamental uncertainty"
into the evaluation.

7.3 Methods for Addressing Parameter Uncertainty in Reasonably Well-Accepted Models

When uncertainty is less fundamental, deterministic sensitivity analyses that
vary parameters locally within a reasonably small range can be used to represent
possible outcomes. If probability distributions over uncertainty parameters are
known, uncertainty propagation methods such as Monte Carlo simulation
become relevant (Morgan et al., 1990). In this context, value of information
approaches such as "real options" can also be used by regulators to assess how
changing the timing or scale of the regulation will improve expected economic
returns (Farrow, 2004).

7.3.1 Deterministic Sensitivity Analysis

Deterministic sensitivity analyses are the most common form of uncertainty
evaluation in regulatory BCA. A relatively few parameters are varied locally,
often one-at-time, over an empirically plausible range.[52] This kind of analysis
indicates the robustness of conclusions about the net-benefits of the regulation,
and which variables are more or less significant for the results. When results are
sensitive to relatively small ranges in parameter values, and have significant
consequences, more information can be gathered to try to better characterize the
uncertainties. Variables that are less significant to outcomes might be taken as
constant, or their values limited to a restricted range.

Varying parameters independently gives misleading information if parameter values are correlated. In the baseline trajectory, for example, the level of
air emissions and the valuation of the associated damage are correlated with
economic growth. In such cases, parameter combinations should be jointly
varied.

---

[52] This approach is conceptually similar to the common comparative static exercise that uses partial
derivatives evaluated at local equilibria to assess the effects of parametric changes on the
model's outputs.

In deterministic sensitivity analyses, the number of possible outcomes increases at the rate of X^n, where X is the number of levels of each parameter and n is the number of parameters. Lacking information about probabilities, the large number of possible outcomes becomes difficult to interpret.

A "scenario analysis" provides a way to reduce the dimensionality of the many cases that can arise from deterministic sensitivity analysis. In the context of the analysis of less fundamental uncertainty, scenario analysis involves choosing representative parameter combinations that give lower, medium, and higher NPVs spanning a "reasonable" range.[53] It is necessary to consider possible covariances among parameters when constructing these scenarios. Analysis designs can be used to eliminate largely redundant parameter combinations to facilitate the choice of parameter clusters that differ in informative ways.

An important problem with deterministic analyses is that the probability of boundary cases is very low. Cooke (2010) gives an example of twenty variables with uniform distributions that vary between zero and one. When these are summed, the maximum possible value is twenty and the minimum is zero. However, if the variables are independent, there is only a 0.1 percent (1/1,000 chance) that the sum is less than 6.07 or greater than 13.9.[54] If the variables are correlated with $\rho = .5$, the range increases to from 2.09 to 17.8. If variables 1–10 have a negative dependence of −0.9 with variables 11–20, the range decreases to 8.71–11.3. Thus, bounding analyses are likely to significantly overstate the range of likely outcomes.

7.3.2 Uncertainty Propagation Methods

Lack of probability information leads to indeterminate policy recommendations using sensitivity analyses unless NPVs are uniformly positive or negative across parameter variations. When parameters have known probability distributions, uncertainty propagation methods solve this problem. Probability distributions for uncertain input variables can be traced through a model to give an outcome probability distribution.

If forecasts of regulatory effects are based on a linear combination of uncertain input variables (as in the example from Cooke 2010 cited above), means and variances of regulatory outcomes can be analytically computed from the expected values and variances of the input variables (Morgan et al., 1990).

---

[53] The term "scenario analysis" is construed somewhat differently in the literature on decision-making under fundamental uncertainty, as discussed in the next subsection.

[54] By the central limit theorem, the summed distribution is normal, so these ranges reflect the probability mass from a normal distribution.

However, the outcomes of AEC regulations are likely to reflect nonlinear combinations of random variables. In this case, Monte Carlo simulation can trace the input probability distributions into a NPV outcome distribution. This allows probabilistic statements to be made about the sign of NPV. If regulatory alternatives are being compared, tradeoffs between the expected value and variance of the alternatives can be considered.

The main implementation difficulty with Monte Carlo simulation is obtaining empirical information about the input probability distributions. The boundary points on the distributions and the distributions themselves matter (Cooke, 2010). In a study by Pindyck (2013), three different distributions are considered for the climate sensitivity parameter used in IAM models: a gamma distribution, a Frechet distribution, and a distribution derived in Roe and Baker (2007). The distributions are calibrated to have the same mean and variances, and the same minimum point as the gamma distribution. The resulting WTP values to avoid threshold global temperature change vary significantly for these distributions.

Using Monte Carlo simulation when empirical distributions are not well known gives an artificial sense of precision. Probabilistic statements about NPVs will be less informative than they appear. This is a common problem in empirical work.

7.3.3 Real Options

The "real options" approach takes advantage of the value of information revealed over time (Farrow, 2004). Real options are relevant in a decision-making context with three conditions: (1) choices about the timing and/or the scale of decisions are flexible; (2) taking actions in the present imposes sunk costs; and (3) future costs or returns are uncertain. The possibility of delaying the decision under these conditions gives the flexibility to decide against initiating an action if future conditions turn out to be unfavorable, thus avoiding sunk costs that would otherwise be unrecoverable, and the losses associated with low-valued future returns. On the other hand, if conditions turn out to be favorable, the action can be initiated. The additional information associated with flexible timing has value, analogous to the price of a "call option" in financial markets. Lacking financial markets, the "real" options that arise from specific decision contexts can be computed, and the associated opportunity cost of lost information from taking a present-period action incorporated into a modified NPV criterion (Dixit et al., 1994). Given a probability distribution of outcomes, this value is estimated from a comparison of the expected NPV of delaying the decision and acting only if the outcome is favorable, against the expected NPV of taking the decision in the present. The difference gives the value of the option to learn about the future. This value is sensitive to the parameters of the model and can be positive or negative (Dixit et al., 1994).[55] That is, the possibility of learning from delaying the decision does not always justify waiting.

The real options framework is often employed in benefit-cost analyses of infrastructures, such as in investments in transport projects (Ministry of Transport, 2016). Regulations fulfill two of the criteria for the application of real options; compliance costs are at least partially sunk, and future costs and returns are uncertain. However, implementation schedules are not always flexible. Implementation schedules are sometimes specified in law. Additionally, political controversies or, in the United States, legal challenges to the regulatory decision and subsequent judicial decisions, have the potential to significantly changes the planned implementation schedule. Unanticipated changes to the timing of regulation pose challenges for both conventional BCA and the use of real options.[56]

7.4 Methods When Uncertainty Is More Fundamental

When uncertainty is more fundamental, two general methods can be used to support decision-making. Research synthesis summarizes knowledge from evolving research or expert judgments about uncertainties such as the health effects of PM2.5 or the risks of catastrophic climate change. A variety of precautionary decision criteria and/or modeling methods can also be used to inform decision-making. These approaches are discussed in the next section.

7.4.1 Research Synthesis

Systematic reviews, meta-analyses, and expert elicitation are three methods for research synthesis (Fann et al., 2016). Systematic reviews produce a qualitative judgment about the implications of research literatures for a well-defined question, such as the magnitude of the C-R coefficients linking exposures to health or environmental risks. As an example, the US Clean Air Act mandates "integrated science assessments" every five years to reassess the health effects of regulated pollutants to inform decision-making about the possible need for the revision of ambient standards.

Systematic reviews are based on well-defined protocols for literature review and study selection (e.g., relevance, credibility, and the weight the study should have in the overall judgment), data extraction and coding, documentation, and

---

[55] Stochastic dynamic programming is used to estimate options in multiperiod models (Dixit and Pindyck, 1994).

[56] Krutilla and Alexeev (2012) show how political risks and costs affect the conventional benefit cost criterion.

reporting guidelines (Fann et al., 2016; Gurevitch et al., 2018). Research from different disciplines that are relevant are included in the studies reviewed. For example, EPA's integrated science assessments include mechanistic, toxicologic, clinical, and epidemiologic studies (Fann et al., 2016).

A meta-analyses can be performed as a second stage of systematic review if the review yields relevant and usable quantitative information (Gurevitch et al., 2018). Or a meta-analysis of a research field can be performed stand-alone. Protocols for literature review, study screening, data coding, transparency and the like are important in meta-analyses. The first step is to extract and standardize "effect sizes" from the studies. Considering the effect sizes from a number of studies increases the sample size. Effect sizes are then entered into a statistical model to estimate measures of central tendency and the influence of heterogeneities. Methodology issues are many, and the subject of an enormous literature.[57] As noted in Section 4, the value of the VSL that the US EPA uses is based on a meta-analysis of stated and revealed preference studies.

"Expert elicitation" is another method for research synthesis. This method can be used when the research literature is relatively sparse. The opinion of experts is solicited in a structured exercise to reveal judgments about parameter values that are fundamentally uncertain. The number of experts not uncommonly ranges from six to twenty-four (Morgan, 2014). Experts can be asked to give estimates of the quintiles or quartiles of a probability distribution. Or they can be asked to provide judgments of a low, middle, and high estimate – the information needed to calibrate a triangular distribution. The degree of variance in expert judgments gives a sense of the state of uncertainty in a research field.

Experts' distributions can be combined to form a "consensus distribution" using a Monte Carlo simulation that draws values from each of them (Krutilla et al., 2015). When combined, the experts' judgments can be equally weighted, or asymmetrically weighted. In the latter case ("the classical method"), the experts are scored on a set of calibration questions relevant to the subject of the elicitation, and the performance scores are used to weight experts' judgments when their distributions are combined (see Colson and Cooke, 2018).

It can be informative to learn whether disciplinary or philosophical differences give rise to different judgments, in which case, combining expert judgments can lose information, and conceivably, muddle the interpretation of the combined distribution. Although not an expert elicitation, a famous survey by Weitzman (2001) of 2,160 economists' recommended discount rates illustrates this issue. The responses were shown to be well described by a gamma distribution. Yet, it is likely that the opinions of the surveyed economists reflected the

---

[57] See Gurevitch et al. (2018) for a review of the field.

several discounting perspectives described in Section 5. In which case, it seems more informative to combine judgments over the relevant subsets of philosophical or disciplinary views and report the results accordingly, rather than to combine asymmetric and not-necessarily consistent philosophical views into one distribution.[58]

7.4.2 Precautionary Decision Criteria and Modeling Deep Uncertainty

Precautionary decision criteria and/or deep uncertainty modeling methods are used when information is too poor to make reliable forecasts and the consequence of being wrong are extremely high and/or irreversible. In this case, traditional forecasting methods provide misleading precision about the possible outcomes of policy actions. As noted in Section 4, some researchers believe that using IAMs to generate SCC forecasts manifests this problem (Morgan et al., 2017; Pindyck, 2017; Stern et al., 2022).

"Minimax" and "minimax regrets" are two decision criteria that can be used when uncertainties are fundamental. These criteria could be relevant, for example, in the decision-making to set safe minimum standards for allowable carbon emissions. The minimax principle requires choosing the decision that gives the best worst case across uncertain futures. It is a conservative criterion that limits the downside risk associated with the decision-making and provides clarity about the worst possible consequences that could follow from a chosen policy.

An alternative is the minimax regret criterion from Savage (1954). This criterion is based on a retrospective thought experiment. If a decision made ex ante turned out to be the best decision for a given state of the world, one would have no regrets. Decisions giving different outcomes would impose a regret as the difference from the no-regrets level. The decision criteria is to choose the policy that gives the lowest maximum regret across possible states of nature. This criterion admits the possibility of worse outcomes than the minimax criterion, but also allows for upside potential to influence the decision-making if better states of the world occur.

A class of "robustness-based" modeling methods have been developed to support decision-making under fundamental uncertainty.[59] These methods have generally been employed at the design stage of a plan or policy, for example, to support decision-making to achieve water supply and management objectives in dry regions facing uncertain climate change (Lempert et al., 2013). To our knowledge, these methods have not been used to evaluate AEC regulations. But robustness-based methods would seem to be promising as a tool to support carbon

---

[58] See Morgan (2014) for a discussion of this issue and others arising in expert elicitations.
[59] See Bartholomew and Kwakkel (2020) for a comparison of methods.

emissions targets consistent with a "safe minimum standard," to help design regulatory standards to give reasonable confidence that NPVs would be positive, or to give reasonable confidence that NPVs of a proposed regulation would be greater than zero, given fundamental uncertainties facing the economic evaluation.

The premise of robustness-based methods is that, when uncertainty is fundamental, all forecasts turn out to be wrong. Applying optimization models to future conditions that will not materialize is not meaningful. Using expected value approaches or uncertainty propagation methods does not solve this problem. For example, Monte Carlo simulation gives misleading results when the model itself is uncertain and parameter values are unknown (Pindyck, 2017). In this environment, the goal of robustness-based methods is to design policies that allow stakeholder-defined performance objectives to be obtained within a reasonable tolerance range (a "satisficing" criterion) in the face of many possible uncertain futures (Lempert et al., 2013).

Using RDM as an example, computer models would generate ensemble forecasts of many possible future associated with a policy action. If the goal was to define a safe minimum level for carbon emissions restrictions, for example, hundreds of thousands of scenarios for global temperatures would be simulated for the considered emissions target, based on different parameter combinations. The range of parameter values must be broad enough to include possible outliers, for example, tipping point thresholds and climate feedback dynamics.

Data mining techniques would then be used to extract a discussible number of scenarios that would have the largest negative effect on the performance objective, for example, result in excessively high global temperatures. This step reveals the parameter combinations to which failure is most sensitive. The next step is to change the policy to attempt to address the problem. For example, an emissions target could be made more restrictive, or a regulatory design could be improved to reduce emissions further. This new policy would be tested for robustness in a new round of simulations. This process would continue until enough of the vulnerability to unacceptable performance had been eliminated for decision-makers to judge the policy approach to be satisfactory. Using a modeling experiment, Lempert and Collins (2007) show that RDM is less conservative than the minimax criterion and more conservative than an expected value optimization.

8 Conclusion

This review considers the application of BCA for the evaluation of regulations that improve air quality, save energy, or reduce climate risks. We started with an overview of the evolution of regulatory benefit-cost analysis, and then covered academic scholarship as well as RIA practice in five key areas: cost analysis, benefit valuation, discounting, distributional analysis, and uncertainty evaluation. Here we offer some concluding remarks about each of these topics.

8.1 RIA Evolution

The integration of BCA into regulatory evaluation has varied in different parts of the OECD, reflecting different proportionality requirements for the use of RIA, and different traditions for using environmental BCA to evaluate regulations and policies. The use of regulatory BCA seems likely to increase with additional policymaking in the air, energy, and climate policy areas, given the significance of the resource tradeoffs. Methods will continue to evolve as the demand for regulatory analysis continues to grow.

8.2 Cost Analysis

Methods for regulatory cost estimation differ in the degree to which regulatory characteristics, market behavior, and market distortions are represented. Engineering cost data are used to specify the abatement costs of differentiated regulations having a relatively limited impact on the overall economy, and engineering cost estimation remains the modal method in RIA. Regulations that have a significant sectoral or economy-wide impact can justify the resources for constructing partial or GE models that explicitly represent the effects of market adjustments and economic distortions.

The welfare costs of GE feedbacks with market distortions are well documented in the literature. The welfare costs of tax interactions in perfectly competitive models dominate the research; the effects of imperfectly competitive market structures are also studied. Tax interactions and imperfect competition do not necessarily affect regulatory cost estimates in the same direction. In general, the selectivity of model specifications and the focus on particular distortions gives an incomplete picture of the direction and magnitude of the totality of GE effects that could plausibly arise from more general specifications in economies with multiple distortions. Existing research suggests that adding environmental quality nonseparably in utility, adding environmental quality to production, and modeling imperfect labor markets, terms-of-trade effects, and externalities in nonregulated sectors, among other distortions, would help fill in the GE picture. Given the challenges of modeling these factors simultaneously, research on the most high-valued modeling improvements would likely to be useful.

For the most part, the literature on regulatory cost estimation does not address implementation frictions, transactions costs, or the costs associated with rent-seeking and/or policy contestation. Inframarginal rents on regulated pollution are significantly larger than abatement costs unless the level of regulation is stringent; thus, public choice models often show that rent-seeking and political competition impose larger costs than conventionally-measured efficiency costs that are manifest at the margins. Rent-seeking and contestation costs are particularly relevant for carbon restrictions, which have visible impacts on energy prices, and generate sizable rents with observable allocation tradeoffs. The implications of transaction costs and policy contestation on regulatory cost estimates would be useful subjects for future research.

8.3 Benefits

In RIA practice, the benefit and costs of AEC regulations are separately estimated, and market prices, market price-derived shadow prices, or benefit transfers like the VSL are used to value outcomes. Representing preferences for health or environmental quality nonseparably in utility functions in a CGE model, and adding environmental inputs into production functions, would allow the integration of BCA within a conceptually consistent GE framework. Policy-relevant spatial heterogeneities, such as local exposure risks and demographic characteristics, would also need to be represented in this model. Making these adjustments comprehensively enough to be relevant for the evaluation of many kinds of regulations, however, is likely to be difficult for routine practice for the foreseeable future.

The value of reducing mortality risks (VSL) and the price of carbon are two major subjects of debate in the benefit valuation literature. The efficiency and equity implications of disaggregating VSL estimates by income, age, and other attributes are important, but commonly elided in RIA practice due to philosophical and political challenges. Regarding carbon pricing, two valuation methods represent different views on the appropriate role of economic evaluation for supporting climate policy. Using the SCC implies confidence in the capacity of IAMs to forecast the value of long-run climate damages, the belief that discounting is appropriate for representing intergenerational tradeoffs, and the view that BCA should be used to determine the level of greenhouse gas emissions. Proponents of the target-consistent approach are more likely to doubt the reliability of long-run damage valuations, believe that safe margins, in the form of precautionary emissions targets, are normatively justified, and support a deliberative process for establishing carbon emissions targets to address intergenerational equity concerns. In this framework, economic evaluation plays the role of cost-effectiveness analysis that guides the lowest-cost emissions trajectory consistent with the policy goal.

8.4 Discounting

The SOC and the CDR are commonly recommended. The CDR is commonly specified using a riskless rate from the bond market or derived from a social welfare function consistent with a Ramsey economic growth model. The SOC is taken as the real before-tax return on capital and can be derived from national income accounts, giving a rate that embodies an economy-wide average risk premium.

Discounting perspectives in the academic literature are reflected in the guidance documents of different countries. European governments tend to use CDRs with riskless rates in the 1 percent to 3 percent range. Risk premia are often added to these rates. Canada and Latin American Countries usually use SOC-based discount rates, varying from 6 percent to 10 percent. In the past, the United States has used a 3 percent CDR and a 7 percent SOC, but discount rate guidance is under review at the time of this writing.

The intergenerational discounting literature shows that uncertainties about the discount rate or the rate of economic growth can cause declining discount rates over time. The discount rates in European guidance documents decline as step functions over successive time intervals, reflecting the belief that longer range impacts should be discounted at relatively low rates.

The positive discounting literature based on market rates is motivated from infrastructure finance, where capital costs are sourced through borrowing. This literature does not represent regulatory cost incidence very well, given that regulations are financed off-budget through economic adjustments throughout the economy. To capture the extent to which regulations induce economic actors to trade present for future consumption, an economy-wide view is needed. The structural details of credit markets (segmentation and credit constraints) that influence consumer discount rates should be represented in this picture.

The intergenerational discounting literature reflects the point of view that discounting is an appropriate way to address intergenerational tradeoffs. An alternative is to use intergenerational transfers to address intergenerational equity, while using the discount rate to efficiently ration capital in the present.

The implications of regulatory cost incidence for the discount rate and the use of transfer to address intergenerational equity have not received much attention in the literature on environmental BCA. These would be worthy topics for future research.

8.5 Distributional Assessment

Environmental regulations impose uncompensated losses on producers, workers, and consumers. The relative burden of environmental regulations on capital and labor is ambiguous in the literature, as is the impact on sector and economy-wide employment. The empirical characteristics of market structure and the type of regulation affect factors returns and employment levels, and the degree to which producer burdens are passed on to the consumer side of the market.

The literature is relatively inconclusive about the distributional impact of regulations on consumer expenditures. Income-class burdens reflect the policy instrument (tax or performance standard), type of fuel, and institutional factors, such as the indexing of transfer payments to the price level. Heterogeneities also affect household fuel consumption patterns holding income constant. These include household characteristics (e.g., age of residents), local climate conditions, transportation options, and commuting patterns. The price and sources of energy also vary regionally. These factors introduce horizontal distributional differences that are as policy relevant as the vertical distributional impacts of regulations.

The distribution of pollution rents or the use of transfer payments can affect the incidence of regulatory burdens. Also, the capitalization of environmental benefits in property valuations can shift the incidence of local air quality benefits between tenants and landlords.

The full dimensionality of this distributional pattern is hard to represent in RIA, and distributional assessments tend to be relatively limited. Impacts on key constituencies, such as labor in the regulated sector, or small business, are often profiled. This limited recording is likely to miss significant distributional impacts.

CGE model can provide disaggregated surplus measures by income quintiles or deciles that embody all welfare channels. The CGE models can also be linked with bottom-up or PE models to represent sectors or regions in greater detail. The use of CGE models to represent distributional effects may become more common in RIA in the future.

8.6 Uncertainty Evaluation

Strong assumptions about the validity of forecasts are implicit in the use of many applied economic models. Conventional Monte Carlo simulation and traditional sensitivity analyses may not adequately represent forecast uncertainties. Decision-science methods for modeling more fundamental uncertainty are likely to be relevant in many regulatory contexts, especially for regulations addressing climate change. The benefits and costs of expanding the use of fundamental uncertainty evaluation methods in RIA would be a useful area for future research.

In all, the technical challenge involved in the benefit-cost analysis of AEC regulations suggests the need for additional research on the way models are designed, validated, and used to support applied BCA. The uncertainties inherent to the evaluation context also suggest the need for perspective about the information that economic analysis provides for regulatory decision-making. Clarity about the modeling limitations will help decision-makers understand the quality of information that RIA provides.

References

Abito, J. M., 2020. Measuring the welfare gains from optimal incentive regulation. *The Review of Economic Studies*, 87(5), pp. 2019–2048.

Acemoglu, D., Aghion, P., Bursztyn, L. and Hemous, D., 2012. The environment and directed technical change. *American Economic Review*, 102(1), pp. 131–166.

Adler, M. D., 2016. Benefit–cost analysis and distributional weights: An overview. *Review of Environmental Economics and Policy*, 10(2), pp. 264–285.

Allen, M. R. and Frame, D. J., 2007. Call off the quest. *Science*, 318(5850), pp. 582–583.

Andersen, D. C., 2018. Accounting for loss of variety and factor reallocations in the welfare cost of regulations. *Journal of Environmental Economics and Management*, 88, pp. 69–94.

Andersen, K. S., Termansen, L. B., Gargiulo, M. and Gallachóirc, B. P. Ó., 2019. Bridging the gap using energy services: Demonstrating a novel framework for soft linking top-down and bottom-up models. *Energy*, 169, pp. 277–293.

Anthoff, D. and Emmerling, J., 2019. Inequality and the social cost of carbon. *Journal of the Association of Environmental and Resource Economists*, 6(2), pp. 243–273.

Atkinson, G., Braathen, N. A., Mourato, S. and Groom, B., 2018. Cost Benefits Analysis and the Environment: Further Developments and Policy Use. Organisation for Economic Co-operation and Development.

Banzhaf, H. S., Ma, L. and Timmins, C., 2019. Environmental justice: Establishing causal relationships. *Annual Review of Resource Economics*, 11, pp. 377–398.

Barrage, L., 2020. Optimal dynamic carbon taxes in a climate-economy model with distortionary fiscal policy. *The Review of Economic Studies*, 87(1), pp. 1–39.

Bartholomew, E. and Kwakkel, J. H., 2020. On considering robustness in the search phase of robust decision making: A comparison of many-objective robust decision making, multiscenario many-objective robust decision making, and many objective robust optimization. *Environmental Modelling & Software*, 127, p. 104699.

Bartik, T. J., 2015. The social value of job loss and its effect on the costs of US environmental regulations. *Review of Environmental Economics and Policy*, 9(2), pp. 179–197.

Bateman, I. J. and Kling, C. L., 2020. Revealed preference methods for non-market valuation: An introduction to best practices. *Review of Environmental Economics and Policy*, 14(2), pp. 240–259.

Belova, A., Gray, W. B., Linn, J., Morgenstern, R. D. and Pizer, W., 2015. Estimating the job impact of environmental regulation. *Journal of Benefit-Cost Analysis*, 6(2), pp. 325–340.

Belton, K. B. and Graham, J. D., 2019. Trump's deregulation record: Is it working? *Administrative Law Review*, 71, pp. 803–860.

Bento, A., Freedman, M. and Lang, C., 2015. Who benefits from environmental regulation? Evidence from the clean air act amendments. *Review of Economics and Statistics*, 97(3), pp. 610–622.

Bento, A. M. and Jacobsen, M., 2007. Ricardian rents, environmental policy and the "double-dividend" hypothesis. *Journal of Environmental Economics and Management*, 53(1), pp. 17–31.

Bishop, K. C., Kuminoff, N. V., Banzhaf, H. S. et al. 2020. Best practices for using hedonic property value models to measure willingness to pay for environmental quality. *Review of Environmental Economics and Policy*, 14(2), pp. 260–281.

Bollen, J. and Brink, C., 2014. Air pollution policy in Europe: Quantifying the interaction with greenhouse gases and climate change policies. *Energy Economics*, 46, pp. 202–215.

Bovenberg, A. L. and De Mooij, R. A., 1994. Environmental levies and distortionary taxation. *The American Economic Review*, 84(4), pp. 1085–1089.

Bovenberg, A. L. and Goulder, L. H., 1997. Costs of environmentally motivated taxes in the presence of other taxes: General equilibrium analyses. *National Tax Journal*, 50(1), pp. 59–87.

Bovenberg, A.L. and Goulder, L.H., 2002. Neutralizing the adverse industry impacts of CO2 abatement policies: what does it cost?. In *Environmental policy making in economies with prior tax distortions* (pp. 609-650). Edward Elgar Publishing.

Bovenberg, A., 1999. Green tax reforms and the double dividend: An updated reader's guide. *International Tax and Public Finance*, 6(3), pp. 421–443.

Bovenberg, A. L. and Van Der Ploeg, F., 1998. Tax reform, structural unemployment and the environment. *Scandinavian Journal of Economics*, 100(3), pp. 593–610.

Boyle, K. J., Paterson, R., Carson, R. et al. 2016. Valuing shifts in the distribution of visibility in national parks and wilderness areas in the United States. *Journal of Environmental Management*, 173, pp. 10–22.

Bull, R. and Ellig, J., 2017. Judicial review of regulatory impact analysis: Why not the best? *Administrative Law Review*, pp. 725–840.

Burgess, D. F. and Zerbe, R. O., 2011. Appropriate discounting for benefit-cost analysis. *Journal of Benefit-Cost Analysis*, 2(2), pp. 1–20.

Burke, M., Hsiang, S. M. and Miguel, E., 2015. Global non-linear effect of temperature on economic production. *Nature*, 527(7577), pp. 235–239.

Caldecott, B. ed., 2018. *Stranded assets and the environment: Risk, resilience and opportunity*. Routledge.

Cameron, T. A., 2014. Valuing morbidity in environmental benefit-cost analysis. *Annual Review of Resource Economics*, 6(1), pp. 249–272.

Carbone, J. C. and Smith, V. K., 2008. Evaluating policy interventions with general equilibrium externalities. *Journal of Public Economics*, 92(5–6), pp. 1254–1274.

Carbone, J. C., Bui, L. T., Fullerton, D., Paltsev, S. and Wing, I. S., 2022. When and how to use economy-wide models for environmental policy analysis. *Annual Review of Resource Economics*, 14, pp. 447–465.

Carleton, T. and Greenstone, M., 2021. Updating the United States Government's Social Cost of Carbon. University of Chicago, Becker Friedman Institute for Economics Working Paper No. 2021-04.

Cecot, C. and Viscusi, W. K., 2014. Judicial review of agency benefit-cost analysis. *George Mason Law Review*, 22, pp. 575–617.

Chay, K. Y. and Greenstone, M., 2003. The impact of air pollution on infant mortality: Evidence from geographic variation in pollution shocks induced by a recession. *The Quarterly Journal of Economics*, 118(3), pp. 1121–1167.

Christensen, J. H., Lopez, J. A. and Mussche, P. L., 2021. What would it cost to issue 50-year treasury bonds? *FRBSF Economic Letter*, 2021(29), pp. 1–5.

Colson, A. R. and Cooke, R. M. 2018. Expert elicitation: Using the classical model to validate experts' judgments. *Review of Environmental Economics and Policy*, 12(1), pp. 113–132.

Cooke, R., 2010. Bounding versus Uncertainty Analysis. Material Provided by EPA in Response to Questions from the SAB Regarding the Limitations of Bounding Analyses in Quantitative Uncertainty Analyses.

Council of Economic Advisors (CEA), 2017. Issues Brief. Discounting for Public Policy: Theory and Recent Evidence on the Merits of Updating the Discount Rate. chrome-extension://efaidnbmnnnibpcajpcglclefindmkaj/ https://obamawhitehouse.archives.gov/sites/default/files/page/files/201701_ cea_discounting_issue_brief.pdf

Cronin, J. A., Fullerton, D. and Sexton, S., 2019. Vertical and horizontal redistributions from a carbon tax and rebate. *Journal of the Association of Environmental and Resource Economists*, 6(S1), pp. S169–S208.

Cropper, M. L., Freeman, M. C., Groom, B. and Pizer, W. A., 2014. Declining discount rates. *American Economic Review*, 104(5), pp. 538–543.

Dalenberg, D., Fitzgerald, J. M., Schuck, E. and Wicks, J., 2004. How much is leisure worth? Direct measurement with contingent valuation. *Review of Economics of the Household*, 2(4), pp. 351–365.

Damigos, D., Kontogianni, A., Tourkolias, C. and Skourtos, M., 2021. Dissecting subjective discount rates and investment literacy for energy-efficient investments. *Energy Efficiency*, 14(3), pp. 1–20.

Danish Finance Ministry, 2019. Key Figures Catalogue.

Davis, L. W. and Knittel, C. R., 2019. Are fuel economy standards regressive? *Journal of the Association of Environmental and Resource Economists*, 6(S1), pp. S37–S63.

Deschenes, O., Greenstone, M. and Shapiro, J. S., 2017. Defensive investments and the demand for air quality: Evidence from the NOx budget program. *American Economic Review*, 107(10), pp. 2958–2989.

Dietz, S. and Stern, N., 2008. Why economic analysis supports strong action on climate change: A response to the Stern Review's critics. *Review of Environmental Economics and Policy*, 2(1), pp. 94–113.

Dietz, S. and Venmans, F., 2019. Cumulative carbon emissions and economic policy: In search of general principles. *Journal of Environmental Economics and Management*, 96, pp. 108–129.

Dietz, S., Rising, J., Stoerk, T. and Wagner, G., 2021. Economic impacts of tipping points in the climate system. *Proceedings of the National Academy of Sciences*, 118(34), e2103081118.

Dinan, T. and Holtz-Eakin, D., 2003. July. A CBO Paper: Shifting the Cost Burden of a Carbon Cap-and-Trade Program. Congressional Budget Office.

Dixit R. K., Dixit, A. K. and Pindyck, R., 1994. *Investment under uncertainty*. Princeton University Press.

Driscoll, C. T., Buonocore, J. J., Levy, J. I. et al. 2015. US power plant carbon standards and clean air and health co-benefits. *Nature Climate Change*, 5(6), pp. 535–540.

Drummond, M. F., Sculpher, M. J., Claxton, K., Stoddart, G. L. and Torrance, G. W., 2015. Methods for the economic evaluation of health care programmes. Oxford University Press.

Drupp, M. A., Freeman, M. C., Groom, B. and Nesje, F., 2018. Discounting disentangled. *American Economic Journal: Economic Policy*, 10(4), pp. 109–134.

Dudley, S. E. and Mannix, B. F., 2018. Improving regulatory benefit-cost analysis. *Journal of Law & Politics*, 34, pp. 1–21.

Eads, G. C. and Fix, M., 1984. Relief or reform? Reagan's regulatory dilemma. Urban Institute Press.

Evans, M. F. and Taylor, L. O., 2020. Using revealed preference methods to estimate the value of reduced mortality risk: Best practice recommendations for the hedonic wage model. *Review of Environmental Economics and Policy*, 14(2), pp. 282–301.

Fabra, N. and Reguant, M., 2014. Pass-through of emissions costs in electricity markets. *American Economic Review*, 104(9), pp. 2872–2899.

Fann, N., Gilmore, E. A. and Walker, K., 2016. Characterizing the long-term PM2. 5 concentration-response function: Comparing the strengths and weaknesses of research synthesis approaches. *Risk Analysis*, 36(9), pp. 1693–1707.

Farrow, S., 2004. Using risk assessment, benefit-cost analysis, and real options to implement a precautionary principle. *Risk Analysis: An International Journal*, 24(3), pp. 727–735.

Fell, H. and Kaffine, D. T., 2018. The fall of coal: Joint impacts of fuel prices and renewables on generation and emissions. *American Economic Journal: Economic Policy*, 10(2), pp. 90–116.

Ferrey, S., 2013. Environmental law: Examples and explanations. 6th ed. Wolters Kluwer, Law and Business.

Florio, M., 2014. Applied welfare economics: Cost-benefit analysis of projects and policies. Routledge

Flues, F. and Thomas, A., 2015. The Distributional Effects of Energy Taxes. OECD Taxation Working Paper No. 23. OECD Publishing. https://doi.org/10 .1787/5js1qwkqqrbv-en.

Fowlie, M., Reguant, M. and Ryan, S. P., 2016. Market-based emissions regulation and industry dynamics. *Journal of Political Economy*, 124(1), pp. 249–302.

Fraas, A. and Lutter, R., 2011. The challenges of improving the economic analysis of pending regulations: The experience of OMB Circular A-4. *Annual Review of Resource Economics*, 3(1), pp. 71–85.

Friedrich, R., Rabl, A. and Spadaro, J. V., 2001. Quantifying the costs of air pollution: The externE project of the EC. Pollution Atmosphérique, 172, pp. 77–104.

Fullerton, D., 2011. Six distributional effects of environmental policy. *Risk Analysis: An International Journal*, 31(6), pp. 923–929.

Fullerton, D. and Heutel, G., 2007. The general equilibrium incidence of environmental taxes. *Journal of Public Economics*, 91(3–4), pp. 571–591.

Fullerton, D. and Heutel, G., 2010. The general equilibrium incidence of environmental mandates. *American Economic Journal: Economic Policy*, 2(3), pp. 64–89.

Fullerton, D. and Muehlegger, E., 2019. Who bears the economic burdens of environmental regulations? *Review of Environmental Economics and Policy*, 13(1), pp. 62–82.

Fullerton, D. and Ta, C. L., 2019. Environmental policy on the back of an envelope: A Cobb-Douglas model is not just a teaching tool. *Energy Economics*, 84, p. 104447.

Gentry, E. P. and Viscusi, W. K., 2016. The fatality and morbidity components of the value of statistical life. *Journal of Health Economics*, 46, pp. 90–99.

Gillingham, K. and Palmer, K., 2014. Bridging the energy efficiency gap: Policy insights from economic theory and empirical evidence. *Review of Environmental Economics and Policy*, 8(1), pp. 18–38.

Gilmore, E. A., Heo, J., Muller, N. Z. et al. 2019. An inter-comparison of the social costs of air quality from reduced-complexity models. *Environmental Research Letters*, 14(7), p. 074016.

Golberg, E., 2018. "Better Regulation": European Union Style. Harvard Kennedy School, Mossavar-Rahmani Center for Business and Government, M-RCBG Associate Working Paper Series No. 98.

Gollier, C., 2013. *Pricing the planet's future: The economics of discounting in an uncertain world*. Princeton University Press.

Gollier, C. and Hammitt, J. K., 2014. The long-run discount rate controversy. *Annual Review of Resource Economics*, 6(1), pp. 273–295.

Golosov, M., Hassler, J., Krusell, P. and Tsyvinski, A., 2014. Optimal taxes on fossil fuel in general equilibrium. *Econometrica*, 82(1), pp. 41–88.

Goulder, L. H., Parry, I. W., Williams III, R. C. and Burtraw, D., 1999. The cost-effectiveness of alternative instruments for environmental protection in a second-best setting. *Journal of Public Economics*, 72(3), pp. 329–360.

Graham, J. D., 2008. Saving lives through administrative law and economics. *University of Pennsylvania Law Review*, 157, p. 395.

Grainger, C. A., 2012. The distributional effects of pollution regulations: Do renters fully pay for cleaner air? *Journal of Public Economics*, 96(9–10), pp. 840–852.

Gray, C. B., 1998. Regulatory reform: Past and future. *Natural Resources & Environment*, 12(3), pp. 155–220.

Greenberg, K., Greenstone, M., Ryan, S. P. and Yankovich, M., 2021. The Heterogeneous Value of a Statistical Life: Evidence from US Army Reenlistment Decisions. BFI Working Paper No. w29104. University of Chicago.

Groom, B. and Maddison, D., 2019. New estimates of the elasticity of marginal utility for the United Kingdom. *Environmental and Resource Economics*, 72(4), pp. 1155–1182.

Groom, B., Drupp, M., Freeman, M. C. and Nesje, F., 2022. The future, now: A review of social discounting. *Annual Review of Resource Economics*, 14, pp.467–491.

Gurevitch, J., Koricheva, J., Nakagawa, S. and Stewart, G., 2018. Meta-analysis and the science of research synthesis. *Nature*, 555(7695), pp. 175–182.

Haab, T., Lewis, L. and Whitehead, J., 2020. State of the art of contingent valuation. Oxford Research Encyclopedia of Environmental Science.

Hafstead, M. A. and Williams III, R. C., 2020. Jobs and environmental regulation. *Environmental and Energy Policy and the Economy*, 1(1), pp. 192–240.

Hallegatte, S., Vogt-Schilb, A., Rozenberg, J., Bangalore, M. and Beaudet, C., 2020. From poverty to disaster and back: A review of the literature. *Economics of Disasters and Climate Change*, 4(1), pp. 223–247.

Hammitt, J. K. and Robinson, L. A. 2011. The income elasticity of the value of statistical life: Transferring estimates between high and low income populations. *Journal of Benefit-Cost Analysis*, 2(1). https://doi.org/10.2202/2152-2812.1009

Hänsel, M. C., Drupp, M. A., Johansson, D. J. et al. 2020. Climate economics support for the UN climate targets. *Nature Climate Change*, 10(8), pp. 781–789.

Harberger, A. C., 1962. The incidence of the corporation income tax. *Journal of Political Economy*, 70(3), pp. 215–240.

Harberger, A. C., 1964. The measurement of waste. *The American Economic Review*, 54(3), pp. 58–76.

Harberger, A. C. and Jenkins, G. P., 2015. Musings on the social discount rate. *Journal of Benefit-Cost Analysis*, 6(1), p. 1–27.

Harrison, M., 2010. Valuing the future: The social discount rate in cost-benefit analysis. SSRN 1599963.

Harrison, G. W., Lau, M. I. and William, M. B., 2002. Estimating individual discount rates in Denmark: A field experiment. *American Economic Review*, 92(5), pp. 1606–1617.

Haveman, R. H. and Weimer, D. L., 2015. Public policy induced changes in employment: Valuation issues for benefit-cost analysis. *Journal of Benefit-Cost Analysis*, 6(1), pp. 112–153.

Helfand, G. E., 1991. Standards versus standards: The effects of different pollution restrictions. *The American Economic Review*, 81(3), pp. 622–634.

Helfand, G. and Dorsey-Palmateer, R., 2015. The energy efficiency gap in EPA's benefit-cost analysis of vehicle greenhouse gas regulations: A case study. *Journal of Benefit-Cost Analysis*, 6(2), pp. 432–454.

Helgesen, P. I., Lind, A., Ivanova, O. and Tomasgard, A., 2018. Using a hybrid hard-linked model to analyze reduced climate gas emissions from transport. *Energy*, 156, pp. 196–212.

HM Treasury, 2021. Green Book Supplementary Guidance: Valuation of Energy Use and Greenhouse Gas Emissions for Appraisal. Department for Business, Energy, and Industrial Strategy.

Hoel, M. and Sterner, T., 2007. Discounting and relative prices. *Climatic Change*, 84(3), pp. 265–280.

Hong, C., Mueller, N. D., Burney, J. A. et al. 2020. Impacts of ozone and climate change on yields of perennial crops in California. *Nature Food*, 1(3), pp. 166–172.

Hsiang, S., Oliva, P. and Walker, R., 2019. The distribution of environmental damages. *Review of Environmental Economics and Policy*, 13(1), pp. 83–103.

Jara-Díaz, S. R., Munizaga, M. A., Greeven, P., Guerra, R. and Axhausen, K., 2008. Estimating the value of leisure from a time allocation model. *Transportation Research Part B: Methodological*, 42(10), pp. 946–957.

Jbaily, A., Zhou, X., Liu, J. et al. 2022. Air pollution exposure disparities across US population and income groups. *Nature*, 601(7892), pp. 228–233.

Johansson, P. O. and Kriström, B., 2018. *Cost–benefit analysis*. Cambridge University Press.

Johnston, R. J., Boyle, K. J., Adamowicz, W. et al. 2017. Contemporary guidance for stated preference studies. *Journal of the Association of Environmental and Resource Economists*, 4(2), pp. 319–405.

Jones-Lee, M. W., 1976. The value of life: An economic analysis. Martin Robertson.

Kagan, E., 2001. Presidential administration. *Harvard Law Review*, 114, p. 2245.

Kaplow, L., 2006. Discounting dollars, discounting lives: Intergenerational distributive justice and efficiency, Working Paper No. 12239, National Burea of Economic Research.

Kaplow, L., 2020. A unified perspective on efficiency, redistribution, and public policy. *National Tax Journal*, 73(2), pp. 429–472.

Katzen, S., 2018. Tracing Executive Order 12866's Longevity to Its Roots. George Washington Regulatory Studies Center. https://regulatorystudies . columbian. gwu. edu/tracing-executive-order-12866% E2, 80.

Kaufman, N., Barron, A. R., Krawczyk, W., Marsters, P. and McJeon, H., 2020. A near-term to net zero alternative to the social cost of carbon for setting carbon prices. *Nature Climate Change*, 10(11), pp. 1010–1014.

Knetsch, J. L., 2020. Behavioural economics, benefit-cost analysis, and the WTP versus WTA choice. *International Review of Environmental and Resource Economics*, 14(2–3), pp. 153–196.

Knight, F. H., 1921. *Risk, uncertainty and profit* (Vol. 31). Houghton Mifflin.

Koskela, E., 2001. Labour Taxation and Employment in Trade Union Models: A Partial Survey. Bank of Finland Discussion Papers No. 19.

Koskela, E. and Schöb, R., 1999. Alleviating unemployment: The case for green tax reforms. *European Economic Review*, 43(9), pp. 1723–1746.

Koskela, E., Schöb, R. and Sinn, H. W., 1998. Pollution, factor taxation and unemployment. *International Tax and Public Finance*, 5(3), pp. 379–396.

Krook-Riekkola, A., Berg, C., Ahlgren, E. O. and Söderholm, P., 2017. Challenges in top-down and bottom-up soft-linking: Lessons from linking a Swedish energy system model with a CGE model. *Energy*, 141, pp. 803–817.

Krupnick, A., Morgenstern, R., Batz, M. et al. 2006. Not a Sure Thing: Making Regulatory Choices under Uncertainty. Resources for the Future.

Krutilla, J. V., 1967. Conservation reconsidered. *The American Economic Review*, 57(4), pp. 777–786.

Krutilla, K., 1991. Environmental regulation in an open economy. *Journal of Environmental Economics and Management*, 20(2), pp. 127–142.

Krutilla, K. and Alexeev, A., 2012. The normative implications of political decision-making for benefit-cost analysis. *Journal of Benefit-Cost Analysis*, 3(2), pp. 1–36.

Krutilla, K. and Alexeev, A., 2014. The political transaction costs and uncertainties of establishing environmental rights. *Ecological Economics*, 107, pp. 299–309.

Krutilla, K., Good, D. H. and Graham, J. D., 2015. Uncertainty in the cost-effectiveness of federal air quality regulations. *Journal of Benefit-Cost Analysis*, 6(1), pp. 66–111.

Krutilla, K. and Graham, J. D., 2012. Are green vehicles worth the extra cost? The case of diesel-electric hybrid technology for urban delivery vehicles. *Journal of Policy Analysis and Management*, 31(3), pp. 501–532.

Krutilla, K. and Krause, R., 2011. Transaction costs and environmental policy: An assessment framework and literature review. *International Review of Environmental and Resource Economics*, 4(3–4), pp. 261–354.

Krutilla, K. and Reuveny, R., 2002. The quality of life in the dynamics of economic development. *Environment and Development Economics*, 7(1), pp. 23–45.

Krutilla, K. and Reuveny, R., 2004. A renewable resource-based Ramsey model with costly resource extraction. *Environmental and Resource Economics*, 27(2), pp. 165–185.

Krutilla, K. and Reuveny, R., 2006. The systems dynamics of endogenous population growth in a renewable resource-based growth model. *Ecological Economics*, 56(2), pp. 256–267.

Kuminoff, N. V., Schoellman, T. and Timmins, C., 2015. Environmental regulations and the welfare effects of job layoffs in the United States: A spatial approach. *Review of Environmental Economics and Policy*, 9(2), pp. 198–218.

Laibson, D., 1997. Golden eggs and hyperbolic discounting. *The Quarterly Journal of Economics*, 112(2), pp. 443–478.

Lempert, R. J., Popper, S. W., Groves, D. G. et al. 2013. *Making Good Decisions without Predictions: Robust Decision Making for Planning under Deep Uncertainty*. Santa Monica, CA: RAND Corporation. www.rand.org/pubs/ research_briefs/RB9701.html.

Lempert, R. J. and Collins, M. T., 2007. Managing the risk of uncertain threshold responses: Comparison of robust, optimum, and precautionary approaches. *Risk Analysis: An International Journal*, 27(4), pp. 1009–1026.

Levinson, A., 2019. Energy efficiency standards are more regressive than energy taxes: Theory and evidence. *Journal of the Association of Environmental and Resource Economists*, 6(S1), pp. S7–S36.

Levy, J. I., 2021. Accounting for health risk inequality in regulatory impact analysis: Barriers and opportunities. *Risk Analysis*, 41(4), pp. 610–618.

Li, Q. and Pizer, W. A., 2021. Use of the consumption discount rate for public policy over the distant future. *Journal of Environmental Economics and Management*, 107, p. 102428.

Li, Z. and Sun, J., 2015. Emission taxes and standards in a general equilibrium with entry and exit. *Journal of Economic Dynamics and Control*, 61, pp. 34–60.

Lind, R. C., 1995. Intergenerational equity, discounting, and the role of cost-benefit analysis in evaluating global climate policy. *Energy Policy*, 23(4–5), pp. 379–389.

Liu, L., Rettenmaier, A. J. and Saving, T. R., 2021. Discounting environmental benefits for future generations. *Public Finance Review*, 49(1), pp. 41–70.

Lontzek, T. S., Cai, Y., Judd, K. L. and Lenton, T. M., 2015. Stochastic integrated assessment of climate tipping points indicates the need for strict climate policy. *Nature Climate Change*, 5(5), pp. 441–444.

MacKenzie, I. A. and Ohndorf, M., 2012. Cap-and-trade, taxes, and distributional conflict. *Journal of Environmental Economics and Management*, 63(1), pp. 51–65.

Markandya, A., Sampedro, J., Smith, S. J. et al. 2018. Health co-benefits from air pollution and mitigation costs of the Paris Agreement: A modelling study. *The Lancet Planetary Health*, 2(3), pp. e126–e133.

Marten, A. L., Garbaccio, R. and Wolverton, A., 2019. Exploring the general equilibrium costs of sector-specific environmental regulations. *Journal of the Association of Environmental and Resource Economists*, 6(6), pp. 1065–1104.

Mayeres, I. and Van Regemorter, D., 2008. Modelling the health related benefits of environmental policies and their feedback effects: A CGE analysis for the EU countries with GEM-E3. *The Energy Journal*, 29(1), pp. 135–150.

Melitz, M. J., 2003. The impact of trade on intra-industry reallocations and aggregate industry productivity. *Econometrica*, 71(6), pp. 1695–1725.

Metcalf, G. E. and Stock, J. H., 2017. Integrated assessment models and the social cost of carbon: A review and assessment of US experience. *Review of Environmental Economics and Policy*, 11(1), pp. 80–99.

Miller III, J. C., 2011. The early days of Reagan regulatory relief and suggestions for OIRA's future. *Administrative Law Review*, 63, p. 93.

Ministry of Transport, 2016. *Adaptive Investment Management: Using a Real Options Approach in Transport Planning*. Wellington, New Zealand. www.transport.govt.nz/assets/Uploads/Paper/MOT-Real-Options.pdf

Morgan, M. G., 2014. Use (and abuse) of expert elicitation in support of decision making for public policy. *Proceedings of the National Academy of Sciences*, 111(20), pp. 7176–7184.

Morgan, M. G., Henrion, M. and Small, M., 1990. *Uncertainty: A guide to dealing with uncertainty in quantitative risk and policy analysis*. Cambridge University Press.

Morgan, M. G., Vaishnav, P., Dowlatabadi, H. and Azevedo, I. L., 2017. Rethinking the social cost of carbon dioxide. *Issues in Science and Technology*, 33(4), pp. 43–50.

Murray, B. C., Keeler, A. and Thurman, W. N., 2005. Tax interaction effects, environmental regulation, and "rule of thumb" adjustments to social cost. *Environmental and Resource Economics*, 30(1), pp. 73–92.

Narain, U. and Sall, C., 2016. *Methodology for Valuing the Health Impacts of Air Pollution*. World Bank.

National Academy of Sciences (NAS), 2017. *Valuing Climate Damages: Updating Estimation of the Social Cost of Carbon Dioxide*. National Academies of Sciences, Engineering, and Medicine. The National Academies Press.

Navrud, S. and Lindhjem, H. 2011. Valuing Mortality Risk Reductions in Regulatory Analysis of Environmental, Health and Transport Policies: Policy Implications. OECD. June 17.

Neuhoff, K. and Ritz, R., 2019. Carbon Cost Pass-through in Industrial Sectors. Cambridge Working Papers in Economics No. 1988.

Newell, R. G. and Pizer, W. A., 2003. Discounting the distant future: How much do uncertain rates increase valuations? *Journal of Environmental Economics and Management*, 46(1), pp. 52–71.

Newell, R. G., Pizer, W. A. and Prest, B. C., 2022. A discounting rule for the social cost of carbon. *Journal of the American Association of Environmental and Resource Economists*, 9(5), pp. 1017–1046.

Noe, P. R. and Graham, J. D., 2019. The ascendancy of the cost-benefit state? *Administrative Law Review Accord*, 5, p. 85.

Nordhaus, W. D., 2017. Revisiting the social cost of carbon. *Proceedings of the National Academy of Sciences*, 114(7), pp. 1518–1523.

OECD. 2019. Better Regulation Practices Across the European Union. Oecd. org, March 19.

OECD. 2021. Regulatory Impact Analysis. Oecd.org, August 7.

Olson, E. D., 1984. The quiet shift of power: office of management & (and) budget supervision of environmental protection agency rulemaking under executive order 12, 291. *Virginia Journal of Natural Resources Law*, 4, p. 1.

OMB. 2003. Circular A-4. Regulatory Analysis. Office of the Management and Budget.

Parry, I. W., 1997. Environmental taxes and quotas in the presence of distorting taxes in factor markets. *Resource and Energy Economics*, 19(3), pp. 203–220.

Parry, I. W. and Williams III, R. C., 1999. A second-best evaluation of eight policy instruments to reduce carbon emissions. *Resource and Energy Economics*, 21(3–4), pp. 347–373.

Parry, I. W., Williams III, R. C. and Goulder, L. H., 1999. When can carbon abatement policies increase welfare? The fundamental role of distorted factor markets. *Journal of Environmental Economics and Management*, 37(1), pp. 52–84.

Pérez-Castrillo, J. D. and Verdier, T., 1992. A general analysis of rent-seeking games. *Public Choice*, 73(3), pp. 335–350.

Pindyck, R. S., 2013. The climate policy dilemma. *Review of Environmental Economics and Policy*, 7(2), pp. 219–237.

Pindyck, R. S., 2017. The use and misuse of models for climate policy. *Review of Environmental Economics and Policy*, 11(1), pp. 100–114.

Pindyck, R. S., 2019. The social cost of carbon revisited. *Journal of Environmental Economics and Management*, 94, pp. 140–160.

Pissarides, C. A., 2000. *Equilibrium Unemployment Theory*. MIT Press.

Pizer, W. A. and Kopp, R., 2005. Calculating the costs of environmental regulation. *Handbook of Environmental Economics*, 3, pp. 1307–1351.

Pizer, W. A. and Sexton, S., 2019. The distributional impacts of energy taxes. *Review of Environmental Economics and Policy*, 13(1), pp. 104–123.

Rabl, A., 1999. Air pollution and buildings: An estimation of damage costs in France. *Environmental Impact Assessment Review*, 19(4), pp. 361–385.

Radaelli, C. M. 2020. Regulatory Impact Assessment (RIA). In P. Harris, A. Bitonti, C. S. Fleisher and A. S. Binderkrantz (eds). *The Palgrave Encyclopedia of Interest Groups, Lobbying and Public Affairs*. SpringerLink. https://doi.org/10.1007/978-3-030-13895-0_136-1.

Radaelli, C. M. and De Francesco, F., 2013. *Regulatory quality in Europe: Concepts, measures and policy processes*. Manchester University Press.

Rausch, S., Metcalf, G. E. and Reilly, J. M., 2011. Distributional impacts of carbon pricing: A general equilibrium approach with micro-data for households. *Energy Economics*, 33, pp. S20–S33.

Robinson, L. A. and Hammitt, J. K., 2016. Valuing reductions in fatal illness risks: Implications of recent research. *Health Economics*, 25(8), pp. 1039–1052.

Roe, Gerard H., and Marcia B. Baker. 2007. Why is climate sensitivity so unpredictable? *Science* 318, pp. 629–632.

Rogerson, R., 2015. A macroeconomic perspective on evaluating environmental regulations. *Review of Environmental Economics and Policy*, 9(2), pp. 219–238.

Savage, L. J., 1954. *Foundations of statistics*, 2nd ed. New York: Wiley

Schelling, T. 1968. The life you save may be your own. In S. B. Chase, Jr (ed). *Problems in Public Expenditure Analysis*. Brookings.

Scientific Advisory Board (SAB), 2017. Advice on the Use of Economy-Wide Models in Evaluating the Social Costs, Benefits, and Economic Impacts of Air Regulations. Prepared for U.S. Environmental Protection Agency.

Sijm, J., Chen, Y. and Hobbs, B. F., 2012. The impact of power market structure on CO_2 cost pass-through to electricity prices under quantity competition – A theoretical approach. *Energy Economics*, 34(4), pp. 1143–1152.

Smith, A. E. and Gans, W., 2015. Enhancing the characterization of epistemic uncertainties in PM2. 5 risk analyses. *Risk Analysis*, 35(3), pp. 361–378.

Spezzano, P., 2021. Mapping the susceptibility of UNESCO World Cultural Heritage sites in Europe to ambient (outdoor) air pollution. *Science of the Total Environment*, 754, p. 142345.

Stern, N., Stiglitz, J. and Taylor, C., 2022. The economics of immense risk, urgent action and radical change: Towards new approaches to the economics of climate change. *Journal of Economic Methodology*, 29(3), pp. 181–216.

Sterner, T. and Persson, U. M., 2008. An even sterner review: Introducing relative prices into the discounting debate. *Review of Environmental Economics and Policy,* pp. 61–76.

Stone Sweet, A., 2003. Why Europe rejected American judicial review: And why it may not matter. *Michigan Law Review*, 101(8), pp. 2744–2780.

Sun, F., Yun, D. A. I. and Yu, X., 2017. Air pollution, food production and food security: A review from the perspective of food system. *Journal of Integrative Agriculture*, 16(12), pp. 2945–2962.

Sunstein, C. R., 2012. The office of information and regulatory affairs: Myths and Realities. *Harvard Law Review*, 126, p. 1838.

Sunstein, C. R., 2014. The regulatory lookback. *Boston University Law Review*, 94, pp. 579–602.

Sunstein, C. R., 2020. Behavioral science and public policy. Cambridge elements. Elements in Public Economics, Eds., Robin Boadway, Frank A. Cowell, Massimo Florio. er. *Michigan Law Review*, 101(8), pp. 2744–2780.

Tessum, C. W., Paolella, D. A., Chambliss, S. E. et al. 2021. PM2. 5 polluters disproportionately and systemically affect people of color in the United States. *Science Advances*, 7 (18), p. eabf4491.

Thind, M. P., Tessum, C. W., Azevedo, I. L. and Marshall, J. D., 2019. Fine particulate air pollution from electricity generation in the US: Health impacts by race, income, and geography. *Environmental Science & Technology*, 53(23), pp. 14010–14019.

Toman, M. A., 2017. *Economics and "Sustainability": Balancing trade-offs and imperatives*. Routledge, pp. 145–159.

Social Value UK. 2016. Valuation of a Life.

US Government Accountability Office (US GAO), 2020. Social Cost of Carbon. Identifying a Federal Entity to Address the National Academies' Recommendations Could Strengthen Regulatory Analysis. Washington, DC.

van den Bremer, Ton S. and Frederick van der Ploeg. 2021. The risk-adjusted carbon price. *American Economic Review*, 111(9), pp. 2782–2810.

Viscusi, W. K. 2010. The heterogeneity of the value of statistical life: Introduction and overview. *Journal of Risk and Uncertainty*, 40, pp. 1–13.

Viscusi, W. K. 2018. *Pricing lives: Guideposts for a safer society*. Princeton: Princeton University Press.

Viscusi, W. K., Magat, W. A. and Huber, J., 1991. Pricing environmental health risks: Survey assessments of risk-risk and risk-dollar trade-offs for chronic bronchitis. *Journal of Environmental Economics and Management*, 21(1), pp. 32–51.

Waldhoff, S., Anthoff, D., Rose, S. and Tol, R. S., 2014. The marginal damage costs of different greenhouse gases: An application of FUND. *Economics*, 8(1).

Walker, W. E., Lempert, R. J. and Kwakkel, J. H. 2013. Deep uncertainty. In S. I. Gass and M. C. Fu (eds). *Encyclopedia of Operations Research and Management Science*. Boston, MA: Spring US, pp. 395–402.

Warner, J. T. and Pleeter, S., 2001. The personal discount rate: Evidence from military downsizing programs. *American Economic Review*, 91(1), pp. 33–53.

Weikard, H. P. and Zhu, X., 2005. Discounting and environmental quality: When should dual rates be used? *Economic Modelling*, 22(5), pp. 868–878.

Weisbach, D. A., 2015. Distributionally weighted cost–benefit analysis: Welfare economics meets organizational design. *Journal of Legal Analysis*, 7(1), pp. 151–182.

Weisbach, D. A. and Sunstein, C. R., 2008. Climate change and discounting the future: A guide for the perplexed. *Yale Law & Policy Review*, 27, p. 433.

Weitzman, M. L., 2001. Gamma discounting. American Economic Review, 91(1), pp. 260–271.

West, S. E. and Williams III, R. C., 2007. Optimal taxation and cross-price effects on labor supply: Estimates of the optimal gas tax. *Journal of Public Economics*, 91(3–4), pp. 593–617.

Weyant, J. P., 2008. A critique of the Stern Review's mitigation cost analyses and integrated assessment. *Review of Environmental Economics and Policy*, 2(1), pp. 77–93.

Wiener, J. B., 2006. Better regulation in Europe. *Current Legal Problems*, 59(1), pp. 447–518.

Wiener, J. B. and Alemanno, A., 2010. Comparing regulatory oversight bodies across the Atlantic: The Office of Information and Regulatory Affairs in the US and the Impact Assessment Board in the EU. In *Comparative administrative law*. Edward Elgar, pp. 309–335.

Williams III, R. C., 2002. Environmental tax interactions when pollution affects health or productivity. *Journal of Environmental Economics and Management*, 44(2), pp. 261–270.

Withagen, C., 2022. On simple rules for the social cost of carbon. *Environmental and Resource Economics*, 82(2), pp. 461–481.

Xepapadeas, A., 2005. Economic growth and the environment. *Handbook of Environmental Economics*, 3, pp. 1219–1271.

Acknowledgments

We appreciate thoughtful guidance from Robin Boadway, Frank A. Cowell, and Massimo Florio, the editors of the Cambridge Elements of Public Economics, as well as from the associate editor Chiara Del Bo. We also are indebted to two anonymous reviewers whose comments substantially improved the Element. Additionally, Don Fullerton, Dana C. Andersen, James K. Hammitt, John S. Evans, Anne Smith, and David Good commented on an early draft. Their reviews also added significant value. Last but not least, we appreciate the production and editorial support received from Vibhu Prathima and Julia Ford and the other members of the Cambridge University Press & Assessment production team. Any remaining errors or omissions are the authors' exclusive responsibility.

Cambridge Elements ☰

Public Economics

Robin Boadway
Queen's University

Robin Boadway is Emeritus Professor of Economics at Queen's University. His main research interests are in public economics, welfare economics and fiscal federalism.

Frank A. Cowell
London School of Economics and Political Science

Frank A. Cowell is Professor of Economics at the London School of Economics. His main research interests are in inequality, mobility and the distribution of income and wealth.

Massimo Florio
University of Milan

Massimo Florio is Professor of Public Economics at the University of Milan. His main interests are in cost-benefit analysis, regional policy, privatization, public enterprise, network industries and the socio-economic impact of research infrastructures.

About the Series

The Cambridge Elements of Public Economics provides authoritative and up-to-date reviews of core topics and recent developments in the field. It includes state-of-the-art contributions on all areas in the field. The editors are particularly interested in the new frontiers of quantitative methods in public economics, experimental approaches, behavioral public finance, empirical and theoretical analysis of the quality of government and institutions.

Cambridge Elements ≡

Public Economics

Elements in the Series

A full series listing is available at: www.cambridge.org/ElePubEcon

Printed in the United States
by Baker & Taylor Publisher Services